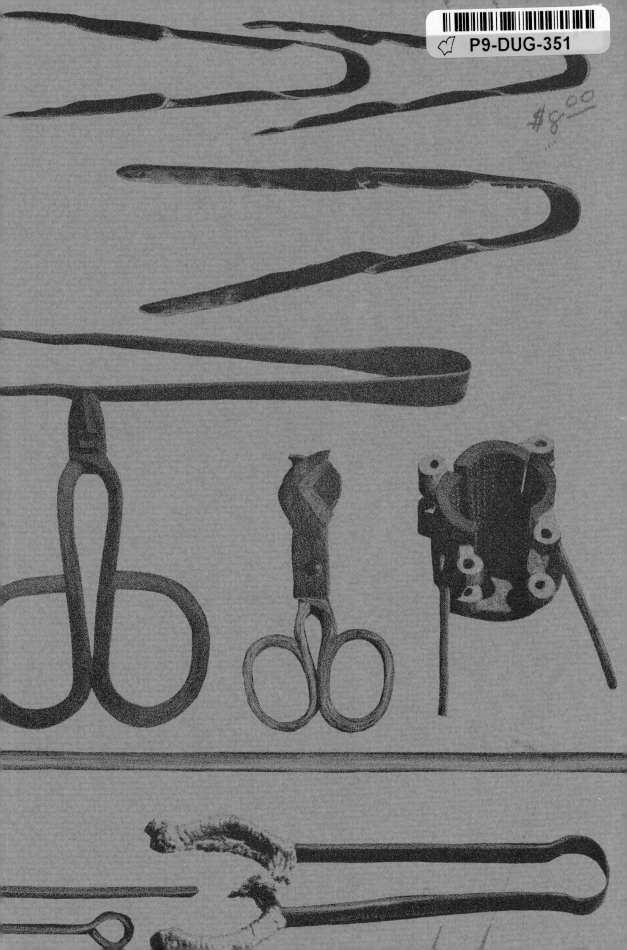

American Glass
Paperweights
and Their Makers

Revised and Enlarged Edition

American Glass
Paperweights
and Their Makers

A story of glass-paperweight
craftsmen of the United States,
their processes, and their products

Jean Sutherland Melvin

Thomas Nelson Inc.

Revised and Enlarged Edition

© 1967, 1970 by Jean Sutherland Melvin

All rights reserved under International and Pan-American Conventions.
Published in Camden, New Jersey, by Thomas Nelson Inc. and
simultaneously in Toronto, Canada, by Thomas Nelson & Sons (Canada) Limited.

Design by Harold Leach

Library of Congress Catalog Card Number: 76–145815

Printed in the United States of America

Dedication

To my husband, George J. Melvin,
and to my sister, Ruth S. Miller
—for their constant help
and encouragement in solving
the problems a work such
as this presents.

Appreciation

So many friends, weight makers, museum curators, collectors, together with librarians, photographers, and typists, have been sincerely interested in the preparation of material for this book and its revision that it is difficult to give adequate credit and sufficient thanks to all for their assistance. Without the untiring help and unfailing encouragement of all these persons this study could not have been attempted.

The craftsmen and their wives who granted personal interviews (or information through correspondence), explained production details, and in some instances supplied valuable photographs of their products include all the craftsmen noted in the text of this book, greatly expanded over the first edition.

Excellent assistance in research was granted by Ruth S. and Thomas G. Miller, Dr. Lony C. and Bertha Thompson, Carl Gustkey, James Moss, Edsel Ford, Alvin Beacraft, Marjorie Plunkett, Alfred E. Knobler, H. J. Claspy, Albert Vottero, Cynthia McDonald, Saranne Finder, Ruth Myers, Winona Taylor, Dorothea Yeager, B. N. Sutter, Ronald L. Gardner, Margaret Heller, William H. Blenko, Jr., J. P. Myers, Mrs. F. J. Sisson, J. A. Guy, Frank M. Fenton, Jr., David Dalzell, Jr., Karel Konrad, Mr. and Mrs. Arnold Constantin, Al G. Smith, and Jack Wiseburn. Librarians and typists who rendered much aid are Mildred Noble, Grace Nuzum, Louise Hudson, Loretta Churney, Sara Johnson, and Vera Jane Conklin. To all these go my sincerest thanks.

For help in securing photographic likenesses of contemporary paperweights despite repeated discouragement I sincerely thank George J. Melvin, Hugh Stevenson, Walter Paget, Dr. William K. Buchanan, and the photography staff of *The Washington* (Pennsylvania) *Observer* including Ronald

Christman, H. B. Hutchinson, James Fuller, Henry Temple, Richardson Photographic Corporation and Color Associates, Inc. Many others who furnished photographs are given credit lines under the reproduction of the specific illustration.

Very valuable aid was given me by the director or curator of a portion of the museums which possess interesting collections of paperweights: Paul Perrot and Kenneth Wilson of the Corning Museum of Glass, Evelyn C. Cloak of the John Nelson Bergstrom Art Center and Museum, Robert De Bartolomeo of the Oglebay Mansion Museum, Mrs. Raymond Bassett, Director, Wheaton Historical Association; by collectors Arthur Gorham, Paul Jokelson, Haven Jones, Franklin and Ramona Knower, Dr. Janius Langston, Celia Vermillion, Amy B. Weimer, and Beatrice Woodward; and by the well-known lecturer and author A. Christian Revi. For seemingly endless hours spent in proofreading and assistance with indexing, my thanks go to Miss Nellie E. Wallace.

Sincere appreciation is expressed to all the above named and to all others unnamed who helped in many ways toward recording the story of contemporary paperweights made in the United States.

Introduction

Current American publications reflect an accelerated interest in paper-weights. This interest is not limited to the fine older European and American weights of the last part of the nineteenth century but includes a thirst for more knowledge of contemporary weights. Research has produced little authoritative material on the contemporary weight makers of the United States. While this book does not propose to be the complete answer to this lack of information, at least a start has been made toward this study.

Family background facts have been included with the story of each contemporary weight maker, that the reader might better understand the man and the training which influences his production. If the style of composition seems elementary, let the reader remember that the author is an elementary teacher, not a journalist, by profession. It is to be hoped that this style will be sufficiently simple to benefit the novice weight collector without boring the well-schooled dealer or collector.

It was my purpose originally to photograph American-made weights and publish black-and-white reproductions of many in this publication. This has proved to be a monumental task which will take much refinement in photography before an adequate guide (via photographs) can be published. Thus, a limited number of illustrations representative of contemporary craftsmen's work is included in this book.

Visiting most of the weight makers, where possible, and corresponding with a very few others has proved to be an enlightening and most pleasurable avocation. Every weight maker is interesting to talk with, congenial, and unfalteringly cooperative in answering numerous and, at times, stupid questions.

In this work every effort has been made to record facts accurately as presented by each weight maker to the author. Each chapter has been checked by the craftsman therein named. There are no finer American citizens, no finer friends than these craftsmen who display an understandably fierce pride in their products. These weight makers desire recognition and appreciation for contemporary products in proportion to the skill and beauty displayed in their execution.

It is to be hoped that this book will help paperweights made in the United States attain a greater degree of appreciative acceptance among serious collectors. Too, perhaps some very unjust misrepresentations can be avoided in future sales of contemporary weights once both salesman and buyer become acquainted with today's weight production.

Note

Because paperweights are made by hand,
all measurements of height, diameter,
and weight indicated in this book
must be considered *approximate.*

A Note
on Paperweight
Identification

Since *American Glass Paperweights and Their Makers* was issued in 1967, I have been called upon by many collectors to identify paperweights. Most of the designs presented for my viewing are vastly different from any weights crafted by contemporary American glassmen—which one may find in a great number of collections today.

I have come to the conclusion that many paperweights were crafted at the turn of this century and shortly thereafter by a vast number of glassworkers of widely varying skills. These were most certainly crafted from the crystal glass furnaces of a great number of glass factories widely distributed over our land by glassworkers who were apparently frequently on the move. Pinpointing these paperweights is an enormous task for a very dedicated researcher. I truly believe that many a fine piece of glass paperweight craftsmanship may never be accurately determined now, just as

Full many a flower is born to blush unseen,
And waste its sweetness on the desert air.
THOMAS GRAY: *Elegy Written in a Country Churchyard*

Contents

Color Plates Follow Pages 32 and 48

Chapter 1

Facts about
Paperweights

During a house tour of beautiful modern homes in our area, one hostess placed in my hands two paperweights explaining, "These are quite old and quite valuable. You know that weight making is a lost art." I could not dispute the words of my kind hostess—nor did I wish to correct her statement before so many awed guests, but I recognized the two prized weights as being made by a weight maker fifty miles distant from her home. Both were finished within fifteen years of that day, yet both indeed were valuable.

There are several active weight makers in America today. It is about these producers who are saving weight making from becoming a lost art in our time that this book is written. Perhaps I am taking a great chance to write about men while they are still living. However, it certainly seems more sensible to me to interview the weight makers, photograph their products, and properly credit their weights while they are living rather than wait until they have passed from the scene and then depend upon others for second-hand knowledge.

Charles Kaziun remarked to me in an interview that the trouble with interviewing friends, relatives, and acquaintances of former glassworkers is that authenticity of identification grows with each inquiry. When first approached about information on a piece of glass or a worker, the flattered friend will say, "Yes, I knew . . . (naming the person). I really don't know for sure, but he *might* have made that glass at . . . factory." At the second inquiry the answer is, "Yes, I knew. . . . Yes, he *probably* made that product at . . . factory." Then by the third inquiry the statement goes, "Yes, I knew. . . . He *made* that product at . . . factory." Thus a glass product is pinpointed to a maker at a specific time and place by the crediting of a well-meaning, close, but sometimes very uninformed friend or acquaintance. It is this type of accrediting I hope to avoid with this study.

While visiting Star City, West Virginia, on one occasion, John Gentile said, "Why don't you write a book about paperweight makers? Nothing has been written recently about American weight making."

John's statement presented the challenge: Who is making paperweights? Where are they? What do they make? This book is the answer to his challenge.

Opinions vary as to the date and place of manufacture of the first paperweight. Some students of glass manufacture say 1820, and some believe that weights were made earlier than that. One group claims that paperweights originated in the glassworks of Murano, Italy. However, it is generally conceded that the finest of all nineteenth-century paperweights were produced in the 1840's at the French factories of Saint Louis, Baccarat, and Clichy. The excellence of these early French weights has rarely been equaled. Some of the early American-made weights rival these beautiful French creations in purity of crystal and distinction of design. The production of our contemporary Charles Kaziun of Brockton, Massachusetts, is judged by many of today's collectors to approximate the beauty and workmanship of these French paperweights.

Paperweights are believed by some to have been called paper holders before they became paperweights. A paperweight may be defined as a rather small, heavy object used to keep papers from blowing away or becoming scattered.

Three sizes of weights according to their diameters are specified as collectible by manufacturers and collectors. They are the miniature weight; the regular, or standard, weight; and the magnum weight. The miniature weight, collected exclusively by some, measures under 2 inches in diameter. Some weight makers specify an even smaller-sized weight as a subminiature. The regular, or standard, weight measures approximately 2 to $3\frac{1}{2}$ inches in diameter. The magnum weight usually measures over $3\frac{1}{2}$ inches in diameter.

Doorstops vary in weight from $6\frac{3}{4}$ to 18 pounds in a variety of shapes. The reader must remember that sizes and weights given are necessarily approximate in handcrafted production.

Weights vary in shape just as much as in size and color. Some contemporary American weights are made in the shape of a sphere. They may be footed or placed on a pedestal. Some are more like a hemisphere with no foot, while others are dome shaped or a flattened hemisphere.

Parts of a simple or dome-shaped paperweight. (1) Base on which weight rests may be flat or concave. It may be coarse ground or polished smooth to eliminate mark where pontil rod was broken off, or it may be cut with a star-shaped design in the bottom. (2) Cushion on which design rests may be clear, colored, or latticinio. (3) Sulphide portraits rest here on cushion. (4) Millefiori canes rest on cushion. (5) Raised design seems to grow from cushion. (6) Air trap is made with piercing tool. (7) Crown is a final gather of crystal glass blocked to enclose all design portions. (8) Some weights receive one or more coats of colored glass known as casing or overlay. (9) Casing is cut away in flat or concave cuts to form windows which reveal the interior design. These windows are called punties.

Common shapes of glass paperweights. *Left to right:* Dome shape, footed weight, pedestal weight.

To understand how an ordinary American glass paperweight is made from a factory pot, one should be aware of its parts.

The *first gather* is a small amount of crystal glass rolled by the maker from the pot of molten glass onto his pontil, a long metal rod. This is the base part upon which each succeeding layer or portion of the weight is formed.

The second part of a weight is the *first color*, called by various weight makers ground, base color, or cushion. This base may be a solid layer of a finely ground color, opaque or transparent, or it may be coarser bits of multicolored glass, called bits, rolled or pressed into the first gather. Today's weight makers frequently add ice-pick air traps to this color layer or manip-

Tools used by a weight maker. *Top to bottom:* Bucket of water for cooling wooden blocking tools. Five variously shaped blocks of apple and cherry wood used to form the shape of a weight. Pontil—a long metal rod on which glass is gathered. Three cut-down tools, also called pucella. Four tools for piercing air traps in molten glass (note ice picks). The die and cup for making a design in the interior of a weight. Shears used to cut off a small or "bit" gather of glass. Asbestos-wrapped holding tongs for lifting completed weight to carry to an annealing oven. (Photograph by George J. Melvin.)

Some weights are marketed with identifying stickers. Shown are (1) Crystal Art Glass, Cambridge, Ohio; Degenhart weights. (2) St. Clair Glass Works, Elwood, Indiana; St. Clair weights, lamps, replica glass. (3) The Pilgrim Glass Corporation, Ceredo, West Virginia; Pilgrim weights, decorative glass. (4) Gentile Glass Company, Star City, West Virginia; personal label of paperweights handcrafted by Mrs. Gertrude Gentile. (5) Zimmerman Art Glass Company, Corydon, Indiana; two types of labels used on weights, lamps, decorative glass.

ulate it with a metal crimp or putty knife. A second gather of glass cases the first color.

The third part of a weight may be added in the form of a *design.* This can take any one of a multitude of forms: a design or lettered motto of finely ground glass sifted into a metal die; a freely formed design of air traps; a design of millefiori canes, glass threads, etc., to mention only a few variations. The most common design made by almost every weight maker in the United States today is called lily. This design resembles the calla-lily flower, which is included three to five times per weight. An air trap centers each flower, representing the stamen.

The fourth part of a weight is the *final gather,* or crown of crystal glass, which encloses the entire weight and seals in all color and air traps.

Our pot weight makers refer to this method of weight making as the layer-on-layer process.

All weights must be carefully annealed to prevent fractures or interior cracks within the designs and to assure continued cohesion of the finished weight. Following removal from the annealing oven, lehr, or muffle (the makers use different terms), weights are ground to smooth off rough places where the weight was cracked away from the pontil rod. Some weight makers fire-polish this pontil mark with a torch prior to the annealing process to eliminate the necessity of grinding. Some weights are ground with flat bottoms, either with very opaque coarse grind or a very fine, highly polished transparent grind, while others are ground and highly polished concave at the bottom.

Few of today's American weights are identified by their makers. Identifications are explained in the various chapters on the makers.

Some of our finest contemporary weights are *overlaid*—that is, cased or thinly coated with one or more colors of glass. These weights are then faceted with straight sides cut on the surfaces, or small concave windows, known as punties (some call them printies), may be ground into the overlay color to reveal the interior design.

What does it take to make glass paperweights?

1. A building. This need not be large, but it should be well ventilated and as nearly fireproof as possible.
2. Fuel. A cheap fuel helps in overall cost of glass production. In many cases glass factories sprang up where natural gas fields were developed. Failure on the part of gas fields sometimes spelled the end of a good glassworks. All of today's pot weight makers use natural gas. The monthly gas bill constitutes a big part of production expense.
3. A secure, day-tank-type of furnace or a good pot. No glass can be melted without a carefully and securely constructed tank or a crucible made of quality prefabricated bricks.
4. A good lead (preferred) or lime crystal mixture. The recipe (without amounts, of course) given me for lime crystal by Mrs. Elizabeth Degenhart follows:

> "Ingredients of batch, lime crystal: sand, soda ash, lime, nitre, borax, potash, manganese, arsenic, powdered blue. All colors of glass have some other ingredient which brings out the color desired. Vaseline glass, for instance, makes use of uranium as the colorant. Bits of colored glass are laid out in various patterns and in the hands of a skilled artisan are incorporated into the crystal and formed into a paperweight," says Mrs. Degenhart.

An interesting note about batch crystals was given me by Bill Reese, former mold shop foreman at Duncan Miller Glass Company, Washington, Pennsylvania. Bill said, "Mixing a batch of crystal glass can be compared to a lady mixing a cake. A recipe is followed exactly, yet each cake turns out differently—just as each glass batch is different. Why? Well, slight variations in raw materials, in the mixing of ingredients, in temperature control, or in any number of minute details affect the final result. No two batches of glass are ever exactly alike. Every glass producer knows on the one hand the joys of good batch crystal or on the other hand the headaches caused by bad batches."

Mr. Reese told me further that competition in crystal production among early American glasshouses was very keen. Recipes were jealously guarded secrets. One story credits the fine quality of Duncan Miller's crystal to an exchange of information between this factory and Fry Glass Company of Rochester, Pennsylvania. Mr. Ernest Miller of Duncan Miller Glass company, an expert in mold making, journeyed to Fry and exchanged his knowledge about molds for Fry's excellent crystal recipe.

5. Good colorants and design materials with cohesion factors compatible with the lead or lime crystal in use.
6. Tools to manipulate the glass. These include:
    a. Pontil rod. A long iron pipe which is also called punty, ponty, puntee.
    b. Marver. A smooth metal plate or even a marble slab on which to roll a gather of glass; used by some for design setup.
    c. Die and cup. To form some designs.
    d. Cradle, workman's bench, or gaffer's chair. A seat with two long arms extending on each side. The seated workman supports and rotates his pontil on these arms while manipulating the hot glass.
    e. Piercing tools—ice pick, metal rods. These are used to make air traps or bubbles.
    f. Cut-down tools, also called pucellas. A series of large metal tweezers used to reduce the size of the glass gather near the end of the pontil ready for breakoff.
    g. A water-filled bucket. Water acting as a lubricant and coolant for the forming blocks.
    h. Blocks. A series of variously hollowed cherry or applewood cups, sometimes with a handle attached. These are used to shape the molten glass into dome, spherical, and other weight shapes as the artisan rotates his pontil along the bench arms.
7. A skilled artisan. Without this all else is naught. Design and workmanship are all important.

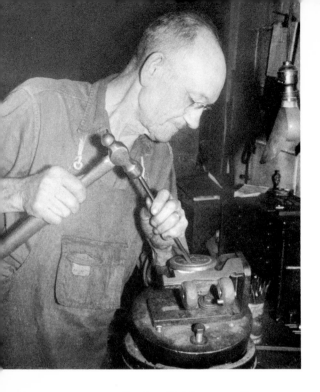

A die plate is handcrafted at C & C Mold Machine Company, Star City, West Virginia. (Photograph by the author.)

8. A reliable annealing process.
9. Grinding, polishing, and finishing wheels to finish the base of a weight smoothly at the pontil break-off point. Some workers use an acetylene torch to fire-polish this breakoff before a weight is annealed.

One important item used in the production of some weights is the die. A visit to the C and C Mold Machine Company of Star City, West Virginia, helped me understand a little of the process for die making. This shop, owned by partners August J. Christoph and Raymond H. Coburn, does a considerable amount of glass mold and die making for the different Morgantown, West Virginia, and Jeannette and Rochester, Pennsylvania, glass companies. These gentlemen explained that it takes from five to six hours to cut a paperweight die in cast iron. All cutting is done by hand with chisels being tapped with repeated blows of a mallet. Of course, all lettering must be done backwards. Dies for paperweights cost from twenty-five dollars up. They have two parts: the die proper is a metal plate in which the design is cut; the cup is the cast-iron cylinder open at both ends with a handle attached to the vertical side on the exterior. This cup restrains the molten glass from flowing beyond the design when the pickup is made.

After the depressions in the die are carefully filled with finely ground particles, the cup which fits quite accurately and is 2 inches or more in height

Steps in making a layer-on-layer weight from a pot of glass using a metal die: (1) and (2) Gertrude Gentile prepares setup of fine powdered glass in die of the famous Gentile Butterfly (patented to Funfrock in 1948). (3) John Gentile makes a first gather from the pot of molten crystal glass. (4) The gather is marvered on a metal plate. (Photographs by the author.) (*Continued*)

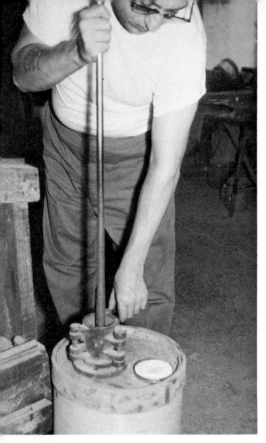
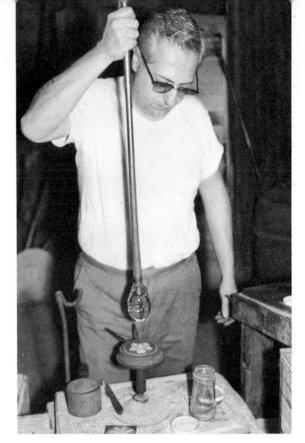

(5) John puts marvered glass into bubble mold and squeezes handle—after which gob is returned to furnace for second gather which traps the air bubbles. (6) The die setup without the metal cup to better show how the second gather picks up the powdered glass design in the die. (7) Cup (sometimes called collar) surrounds the design, then pickup is made. The cup prevents the molten glass from extending beyond the die. (8) After "warming in" the powdered glass of the design, forming is done with the pucella. (Photographs by the author.) (*Continued*)

(9) Butterfly wings are tipped with handle of the tool. (10) Partial cutdown is made at base of weight. (11) John blocks the weight following third gather of glass. (12) Further shaping at base of weight with cut-down tool or pucella. (Photographs by the author.) (*Continued*)

(13) Pontil neck of glass is narrowed.
(14) Final gaffer's inspection allows for slight cooling of the weight.

(15) Weight is ready for breakoff from pontil, accomplished by striking a quick sharp blow of a stick to the pontil rod. Weight falls into sandbox.
(16) Weight on sand table·is slightly cooled before it is carried to annealing oven with asbestos-wrapped tweezers. (Photographs by the author.)

is placed to surround the die plate completely. This cup serves to restrain the molten glass from flowing out of shape as the gather is pressed onto the die to pick up the color design. Other terms used by weight makers to describe the cup are receiver and collar.

No matter how many trips one makes to a weight maker's shop, there is nothing quite like trying to make a weight yourself, as I found out. Because I felt that to write about this subject properly I should experience the process, I asked and was granted permission to try weight making. With considerable coaching and assistance from Gertrude Gentile at Gentile Glass Company, I tried the art of weight making. As in other fine crafts, it is easy to watch, but *hard* to do.

The molten glass cannot be distinguished from pot or gas flame when one looks into the furnace opening, until careful teaching indicates that the pontil rod or punty casts a shadow as it approaches the surface of the molten glass of the batch in the furnace.

A deft twirl of the pontil catches the initial small gather of taffy-like molten glass. This gob is quickly rolled on a table spread with multi-colored glass fragments, then returned to the furnace to "warm in." All the time the pontil must be rotated. This multi-color or initial color, properly heated, is then marvered or rolled on a metal plate in *both* directions to form a conical or cylindrical shape. The conically shaped glass is, in some instances, inserted in the bubble mold for a quick squeeze to insure evenly spaced air bubbles in the weight. A second gather of glass traps these air bubbles. In my case, I was glad to block this second gather, cut down, and break off, but usually the trained worker will further enhance his design with additional colors and a third gather of glass before he blocks, cuts down, and breaks off from the pontil rod.

If nothing else I furnished all those watching the show with a lot of amusement. The heat of the furnace, the exertion of trying to follow the steps of this craft, left me exhausted. However, I am the proud possessor of a "Melvin Special," as John Gentile calls it.

How does one select American-made paperweights for a collection?

By appeal—in beauty, color, design, clarity of crystal, and depth of dome—plus high quality workmanship. Condition, authenticity, and rarity

(1) A "moon-man" made by impressing features in the crystal casing over a color center, the product of Robert Hamon. (2) A pencil holder crafted by Roberto Moretti of the Pilgrim Glass Corporation, Ceredo, West Virginia. This holder, which accommodates eight pens or pencils, is five and one-half inches high and is signed "R. Moretti." (3) A faceted rose weight made by John Murphy at Fostoria Glass Company. (4) A contemporary Steuben weight cases a large five-petal flower over white base color. Collection of Margaret Hellen, Newcomerstown, Ohio. (5) A large flat weight by Jimmy Hamilton cases nine white rods as an underlay for five green and white flowers. (6) A John Murphy weight.

As each Murphy design is unique, it is hard to generalize about them, but they usually are regular size, about three inches. Among the styles he makes are those hand painted on opal glass plates and those with carefully arranged glass bits designed to resemble flowers. No Murphy weights are sold, but are made only as gifts to friends. (7) Tom Mosser has little time to create paperweights at his Variety Glass Company Shop. Shown are two Mosser weights, a multicolor center swirl surrounded by deep air traps and a crimped design cased with blue glass. (8) An experimental sulphide of Prince Albert made by Whittemore. (Photograph 4 by George J. Melvin; all others by the author.)

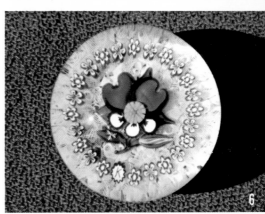

(1 through 6) Kaziun weights. (1) Pansy with bud on alabaster white; tiny bug on lower leaf. (2) Coral red snake on aqua jasper ground. (3) Double pink convolvulus with two buds and bugs on blue diamond trellis on white ground. (4) Sandwich-type red rose and bud on latticinio over amethyst. (5) Sandwich-type roses with striped leaves and gold bug on muslin. (6) Pansy with gold bug on muslin with ring of millefiori canes, signed with K cane. (7) A ringholder and (8) a yellow tomato and a green pepper made at Scott Depot, West Virginia, and sold by Kanawha Glass. (9 and 10) Recent Ronald Hansen designs are the colorful fish setup against a salmon base and a six-petal, multi-colored flower weight with six facets. Collection of Dr. and Mrs. L. C. Thompson. (11) A faceted yellow and brown butterfly on a lavender base by Ronald Hansen. Collection of Jack Wiseburn. (Photographs by the author.)

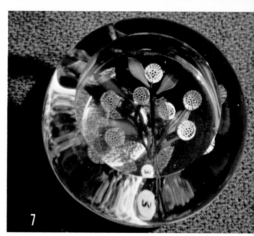

(1 through 10) Francis Whittemore designs. *(1 and 2)* Experimental works, a rose in a wine glass and a small vase encasing pulled design flowers and leaves. *(3)* A colorful spray bouquet of blue, yellow, and rose colored flowers. *(4)* A footed white rose encased in clear crystal and faceted. *(5)* A five-petal yellow flower with bud. Note that there is no color ground. *(6)* A blue rose encased in crystal, overlaid with opaque white. *(7)* Blue ageratum spray. *(8 and 9)* Two weights with rose flashing. *(10)* A pink rose wig stand. Notice the "W" signature in 3, 7, and 8. (Photographs by the author.)

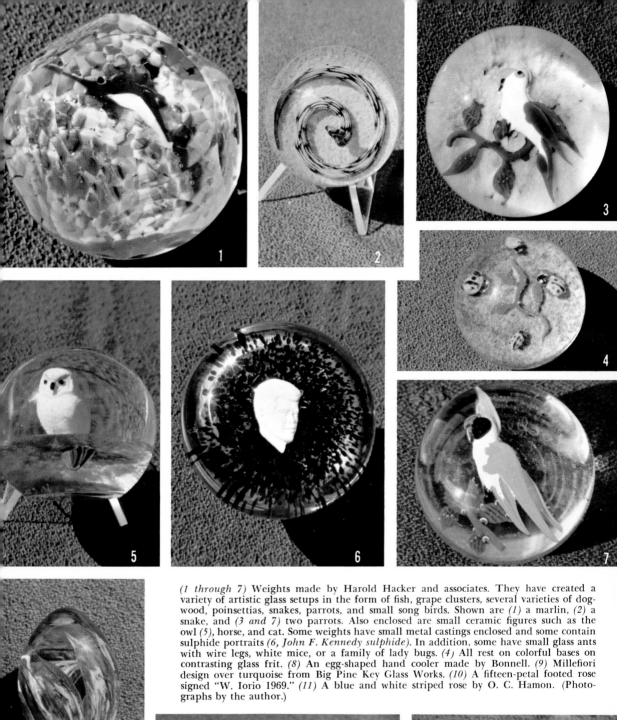

(1 through 7) Weights made by Harold Hacker and associates. They have created a variety of artistic glass setups in the form of fish, grape clusters, several varieties of dogwood, poinsettias, snakes, parrots, and small song birds. Shown are *(1)* a marlin, *(2)* a snake, and *(3 and 7)* two parrots. Also enclosed are small ceramic figures such as the owl *(5)*, horse, and cat. Some weights have small metal castings enclosed and some contain sulphide portraits *(6, John F. Kennedy sulphide)*. In addition, some have small glass ants with wire legs, white mice, or a family of lady bugs. *(4)* All rest on colorful bases on contrasting glass frit. *(8)* An egg-shaped hand cooler made by Bonnell. *(9)* Millefiori design over turquoise from Big Pine Key Glass Works. *(10)* A fifteen-petal footed rose signed "W. Iorio 1969." *(11)* A blue and white striped rose by O. C. Hamon. (Photographs by the author.)

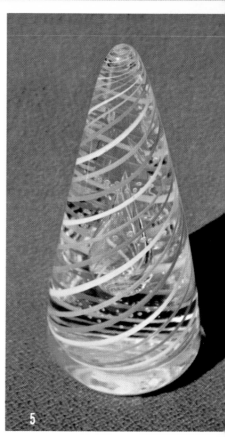

(1) Colorful lamp-work bugs by Henry C. Johnson are enclosed by Gentile against jaspered grounds or leaves of glass frit. (2) A John Degenhart weight also containing a name plate; a hollow John Gentile multi-color weight which was blown into a ribbed mold and topped with a chicken; John Gentile's eight-petal, or spider design, weight with a crystal hen. (3) Devil's fire paperweights. John Gentile red glass swirls in crystal casing and a pink swirled glass weight of unknown origin. (4) Bell-shaped paperweights (left and right) by John Gentile and (center) by St. Clair Glass Works. (5) A wig stand with three colors of glass rods in spiral design made by Peter Gentile. (6) Die weights by John Gentile commemorating the moon landing July 20, 1969. (7) A footed red rose by Pat Naples. (Photographs by the author.)

(1) Imperial Glass Company casts glass paperweights in the forms of a ground hog and owl in crystal or in color. *(2)* A very colorful footed rose crafted by Harry Caralluzzo at Cambridge, Ohio. *(3)* Kent Ipsen doorstop. *(4)* Delicate tulip design built one petal at a time, three to a layer. No crimp is used, as petals are gathered singly from a small pot of color. *(5)* Brilliant grape cluster with delicate green leaves and stems with perimeter millefiori canes. *(6)* Peter Ray-mond doorstop made at the Fenton Cut Glass Company, Williamstown, West Virginia. *(7)* Otto Macho made this weight with three morning glories when he worked at Durand. *(8, 9, and 10)* Frank Hamilton weights. A lovely five-petal pink flower accented with blue millefiori rods over pink and blue base; a six-petal flower; and a weight with flowing colors. (Photograph 3 by Anger Studios, Kenosha, Wisconsin; all others by the author.)

(1 and 2) Paperweights crafted by Nick Labino include a bright red crocus with white overlay cased with pale green glass and a unique weight of six iridescent petals of yellow, gold, and brown cased with blue green. (3) A paperweight with a yellow tulip enclosure by Dominick Labino. The tulip was made freehand from molten glass. (4) An example of Bill Breeden's paperweights—a miniature lamp-glass weight of millefiori rods arranged around a center rod spaced against a contrasting base color. (5) The stopper made by Bill Breeden. (6 and 7) Paperweights made by the lamp process of William F. Breeden. (8, 9, 10, and 11) Joe Barker miniature weights. (8) A six-petal yellow flower on a blue base and (11) two snake weights, signed "Joe Barker." Collection of Jack Wiseburn. (9) A poinsettia-type flower with many pointed petals and (10) narcissus on deep blue ground color. (12) An Ed Rithner bell-shaped weight. (Photographs by the author.)

records of purchase or source of the weights are lacking, so no accurate information is to be had from a visit—only the enjoyment of gazing at the beauty of color and design encased in crystal.

The outstanding example of a museum devoted to the display of paperweights is the John Nelson Bergstrom Art Center and Museum at Neenah, Wisconsin, where over seven hundred weights are included in the collection of the late Evangeline Bergstrom and are artistically spaced, lighted, and displayed, providing leisurely study for the visitor.

The Smithsonian Institution at Washington, D.C.; Corning Museum of Glass, Corning, New York; Toledo Museum of Art, Toledo, Ohio; Old Sturbridge Village, Sturbridge, Massachusetts; Saint Mary's Seminary, Perryville, Missouri; and Saint John's Seminary, Camarillo, California, have larger collections of paperweights. Oglebay Mansion Museum at Wheeling, West Virginia, and the Historical Society of Western Pennsylvania of Pittsburgh, Pennsylvania, are among the several institutions owning a lesser number of weights.

Interest in contemporary weights is growing rapidly. The following chapters are intended to assist the new (and perhaps the seasoned) collector to identify weights made in the United States today.

Part II

The Independent

Pot Workers

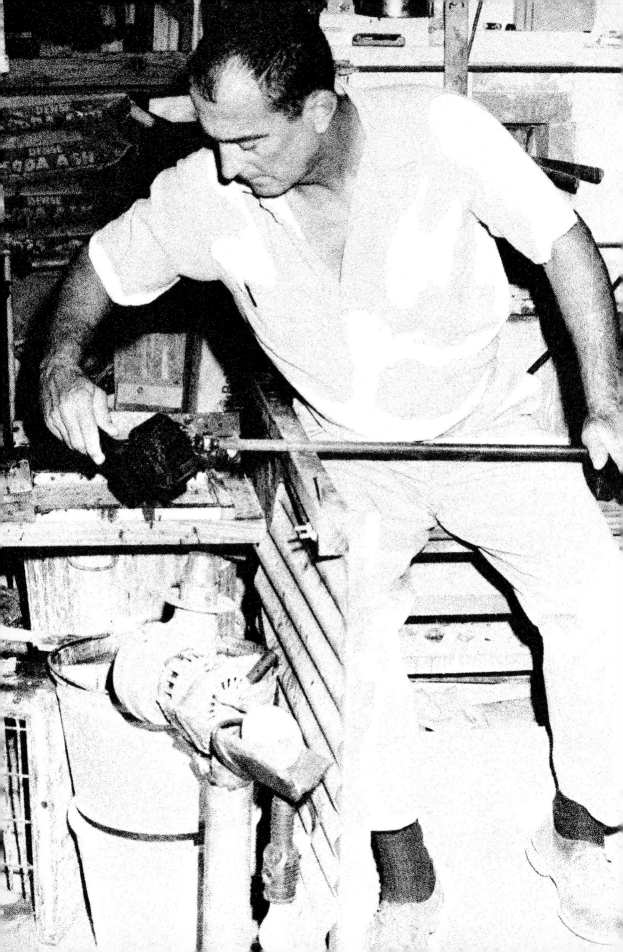

Chapter 2

Lester S. Cunningham,
Big Pine Key, Florida

Located on Big Pine Key is a glassworks by the same name—Big Pine Key Glass Works—operated by Lester S. Cunningham. Situated on U.S. Route 1 one hundred twenty miles south of Miami and thirty miles from Key West, the factory is a big tourist attraction. About one hundred people visit daily even in the off-season.

In the Big Pine Key complex are a gift shop, showroom, and machine, welding, and mold-casting shops. Electric annealing ovens are constructed on the spot for factory use. Also in the complex are a home for Mr. and Mrs. Jennings Bonnell and living quarters for Dennis Klinsky, Henry Whitehair, and Steve Hujo, the staff of glass craftsmen who work in Mr. Cunningham's factory. Mr. Bonnell, age forty-eight, who started glasswork at McBride Glass Company, Salem, West Virginia, thirty-one years ago, also had previous experience at Imperial Glass Corporation, Bellaire, Ohio, before assuming a gaffer's job at Big Pine Key, where he does make some paperweight designs.

Lester Cunningham was born in Philadelphia, Pennsylvania, January 24, 1922, to Harry B. and Edith A. Cunningham. The Cunningham antecedents, in the 1700's, first settled in America in the Boston area where they worked at glazing pottery. Later members of the family worked in the glass industry in both South Jersey and Pittsburgh.

Lester Cunningham crafts a weight. (Photograph courtesy of Lester Cunningham.)

Jennings Bonnell, manager of Big Pine Key Glass Works. (Photograph courtesy of Lester Cunningham.)

A Star of David in blue over white ground made at Big Pine Key Glass Works. (Photograph by the author.)

Three faceted weights. The lower two contain millefiori designs over turquoise base color. (Photograph by the author.)

Ted Whitehair of Big Pine Key Glass Works has also made some paperweights. (Photograph courtesy of Lester Cunningham.)

Two unsigned weights containing three lilies of pale yellow and blue growing from white carpets. (Photograph by the author.)

Two paperweights crafted by Lester S. Cunningham at Big Pine Key Glass Works, Florida. (Photograph by the author.)

Three crimped weights in orange, green, and yellow from Big Pine Key, signed with a triangular die marked BPKGW. (Photograph by the author.)

Cunningham's life story could easily be a subject for a novel. Always attracted to the glass industry, from time to time he worked for the fineglass craftsmen in southern Jersey and throughout Europe without pay just to learn. In India he worked with and studied under Charan, who taught him "to make glass the right way." This experience which Mr. Cunningham considers very valuable came while he, as a graduate engineer, was on big construction jobs scattered throughout the world. Following his years spent in schooling, army duties, deep-sea diving, and in construction, Mr. Cunningham settled near Fort Myers. Here his citrus groves were soon swallowed up by city expansion. In 1961 he moved to the Keys and began

Three seven-petal flowers centered around an air trap over multicolor bases made at Big Pine Key Glass Works. (Photograph by the author.)

to consider construction of a plant for the manufacture of handcrafted glass. The Plant City, Florida, and Pompano, Florida, sands have proved to be good glass sands. Other materials and colorants are secured throughout the United States. This plant has been in operation since 1965.

Lester Cunningham crafts weights including an eagle sulphide. He has rights for a unique "Paperweight-of-the-Month Club" whose members receive, each month, a unique collector's weight. Weights are not mass produced, and designs are made in miniature size through doorstop size. He says, "We now seek to recapture our past craftsmanship. These crafts, mostly dead, were the basis of this nation's overall production today. The buyers we see here are after handmade wares on a level they can live with. We are small in name here, but large in equipment and effort. Our object is, in time, to produce about the best."

Chapter 3

John Degenhart
William Degenhart
Cambridge, Ohio

A glassworker with keen recollection of many of America's fine, early glass plants was John Degenhart of Cambridge, Ohio.

Born at Wheeling, West Virginia, September 5, 1884, John Degenhart was a son of the late Andrew Degenhart (originally spelled Degenhardt), an immigrant from Nuremberg, Germany, and Louise Franc Degenhart. After working as a railroad engineer in Germany, Andrew immigrated to the United States when about thirty-five years of age and found work as a mold maker in one of the early Pittsburgh glass factories. He married a Wheeling lass thirteen years his junior in 1881.

While in Wheeling Andrew Degenhart became a mold maker for Hobbs, Brockunier and Company. Among later molds that he made was one made at the Beatty-Brady Glass Company while he was employed at their factory in Dunkirk, Indiana. This was a mold for the Dewey Commemorative Pitcher. This design contained a series of cannonballs and may be readily distinguished from another Dewey pitcher design.

Andrew and his wife Louise Franc were parents of Charles Degenhart, born 1882; John, born 1884; and Frank, Charlotte, Andrew, and Louis.

Andrew, Sr., removed to Findlay, Ohio, from Wheeling and worked in various factories there and in Indiana until his death in 1901 at fifty-six years of age. He is reputed to have been an excellent mold maker but rarely stayed very long at one factory.

John Degenhart forms a scent-bottle stopper. (Photograph by George J. Melvin.)

Both Charles and John Degenhart became glassworkers at an early age. Between the ages of ten and fifteen, John worked at Dalzell, Gilmore, and Leighton Company. Henry Forger, the Dalzell mold shop foreman, left Findlay, Ohio, to come to Cambridge, Ohio, when the new buildings for the Cambridge Glass Company were being constructed. Through the kindness of Mr. Forger, John Degenhart found work as a laborer at this new plant from November, 1901, until it was opened as a factory in 1902—thence, as a glass apprentice.

John Degenhart's glass-factory training included gathering for the blow shop and blowing. In 1916 he became a presser and worked as head of a shop from that time until he left the Cambridge Glass Company. John explained that during the days of Hoosier Kitchen Cabinets about six weeks a year at the Cambridge Glass Company were devoted to blowing glass jars for these cabinets.

For many years both Charles and John Degenhart had spent after-hours at the Cambridge Glass Company in the production of glass paperweights. Some of the fine examples owned today by Mrs. Elizabeth Degenhart are the product of the combined efforts of these brothers. Mrs. Degenhart assisted, too, with some design ideas.

Paperweight designs made by the Degenharts at the Cambridge Glass Company by 1929 included the following: summer scene, winter scene, president's pictures, names, mottoes, and lodges, all painted on small opaque white plaques and inserted in crystal weights. There were also individual photographs, flower weights, Sandwich Glass Company fragment weights, and morning glory, lily, beehive, bug, hen, rooster, engine, butterfly, and snake designs. Of the snake weights John said, "My brother [Charles] was real good at them snakes. He could do anything with glass threads." An example of a Degenhart snake weight may be seen at the John Nelson Bergstrom Art Center and Museum, Neenah, Wisconsin.

One distinctive weight of Mrs. Degenhart's collection is a lily-type flower encased in crystal. The sparkling fragments used to make the flower were crushed from glass waste at the Cambridge factory. Mrs. Degenhart's story is, "One of the Cambridge glassworks' pots had a 'calf.' In other words, the

A portion of Mrs. Degenhart's collection of weights. (Photograph by George J. Melvin.)

bubbling glass boiled over out of a pot. The spilled glass is called a 'calf.' "
These crystal bits, crushed and then enclosed in the one-of-a-kind weight, have
particular brilliance.

Small crystal bird, bug, butterfly, and animal shapes were coated with
ground glass. Then they were heated and encased in the center of paperweights
of crystal or sometimes in crystal with an overlay of colored glass. Some of the
red, green, yellow, amethyst, amber, and milk-white overlay-over-crystal
weights were then faceted with four windows of parallel sides, or slant-surfaced
windows, which sloped almost to a point at the top. One very unusual overlay
weight is called Moonlight by Mrs. Degenhart. It is a pale light-blue overlay-
on-crystal faceted weight.

Mrs. Degenhart explained why these faceted overlay weights resemble
others made elsewhere in Ohio. One time the town of Cambridge had an arts
and crafts show. Always one to observe new ideas, Mrs. Degenhart saw an overlay, faceted, lily design weight and described it to her husband. Experimentation at the Cambridge Glass Company factory proved that John and Charles
Degenhart could make weights like the one "Lizzie" had seen. These weights
are unusual and highly prized by today's collectors of American weights. An
example of a Degenhart amethyst overlay may be viewed at the Henry Ford
Museum, Dearborn, Michigan.

Degenhart production weights were made in many colors. Only the one on the right was
named—John Degenhart called it Double Tree. (Photograph by George J. Melvin.)

A scent bottle and paperweights made by Charles Kaziun of Brockton, Mass. (Color photographs courtesy of Mr. Charles Kaziun.)

(*Top*) Three steps in making a Gentile five-flower paperweight. (*Center*) Collectors weights made by John Gentile include spiral, flying goose, Old Glory, millefiori, footed red and white rose. (*Bottom*) John Gentile's butterfly with flower, footed red rose weight, miniature flying goose, Old Glory, spiral, and millefiori paperweights. (Photographs by George J. Melvin.)

(*Top*) Zimmerman Art Glass Company paperweights include the popular pear and apple, the unique bubble, pink crocus, and metal butterfly designs. (*Center*) Three collector's weights (all footed) crafted at Zimmerman Art Glass Company include a metal butterfly (glass coated) over blue and white pond lily, large pink crocus, and white crocus in green grass. (*Bottom*) Three production weights from Zimmerman Art Glass Company include eleven ice pick bubble weight, fountain and pond lily designs. (Photographs by George J. Melvin.)

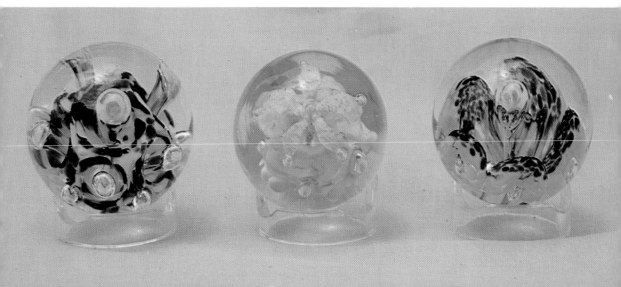

(*Top*) Three footed Whittemore rose paperweights. (*Center*) Paperweights made by William Zick Senior and Junior at the Morgantown Glassware Guild Incorporated, Morgantown, W. Va. (*Bottom*) J. R. Stone's pen and pencil holders and Fowlerton reproduction weight. (Photographs by George J. Melvin.)

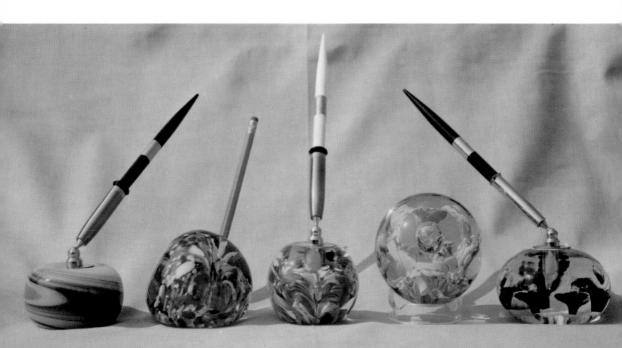

Charles Kaziun weights. *Top:* red rose footed and yellow rose footed; *bottom:* pink rose footed and pleated petal peachblow wild rose.

(*Top*) St. Clair pear, apple, and bell paperweights. (*Center*) St. Clair star and rose paperweights. (*Bottom*) St. Clair ceramic frog, multicolor swirl, and sulphide butterfly weights. (Photographs by George J. Melvin.)

(*Top*) Two doorstops and a bookend made by Ed Rithner. (*Center*) Five weights made by Rithner using dies. Note delicate white petal edging in flower of magnum weight pictured in center. (*Bottom*) Edward Rithner's candy cane and gold ruby, turquoise and cobalt blue five and eight petal, delicately etched in white, flower weights made at Wellsburg, W. Va. Center and bottom weights from the collection of Celia Vermillion. (Photographs by George J. Melvin.)

Ronald Hansen paperweights. Fruit, flower, and snake.

(*Top*) Two cane weights by Stelzer and a Sommers swirl (center). (*Left*) Peter Raymond's pink flower weight with cane stamen. From the collection of James Moss. (Photograph by the author.) (*Bottom*) Emil Kuhn's crimp weight made at the Morgantown Guild factory in Morgantown, W. Va.; a beautiful gold ruby red rose paperweight made by Emil Larson (from the collection of James Moss); and a William E. Claytor decal weight. (Photographs by George J. Melvin.)

(*Top*) Three footed rose paperweights made by John Degenhart. (*Center*) Degenhart products include rose stopper scent bottle, window weight, gear shift knob, plaque name weight, footed yellow rose weight, and bookend. (*Bottom*) A Degenhart bookend with fluted base and two scent bottles. (Photographs by George J. Melvin.)

(*Top*) Peter Gentile weights. The butterfly with cane body dates this as being made prior to the 1948 Funfrock patent. (*Center*) Three examples of Gertrude Gentile's craftsmanship. (*Bottom*) Erickson weights. Three green lily over gold ground; cranberry bubble weight; and three amethyst lily over gold color ground. From the collection of Mr. and Mrs. Franklin Knower. (Photographs by George J. Melvin.)

Charles Kaziun paperweights. Red tulip; blue crocus; yellow over pink rose; yellow jonquil; red pleated petal dogwood.

Four types of crystal forms used by John Degenhart were the squirrel, butterfly, bee, and chicken. The solid crystal shapes were coated with fine glass and then enclosed in spheres of crystal, sometimes resting upon, sometimes flying above, a cushion of varicolored glass bits. (Photograph by George J. Melvin.)

Degenhart crimp weight and matching scent bottle. Opaque white with red and blue combined to make these products. (Photograph by George J. Melvin.)

Degenhart rose weights were made in a variety of color combinations. This group includes a rose and white, all white, all yellow, and blue-and-white striped rose. All are footed weights except the white one. (Photograph by George J. Melvin.)

After working for the Cambridge Glass Company for forty-six years, John Degenhart decided to open his own factory. In a concrete block structure that he built expressly for small glass job production, John opened for business the first week of May, 1947, under the name Crystal Art Glass Company. John's factory worked annually five months out of each calendar year.

Freddie Apple of Newark, Ohio, had been urging John Degenhart to start his own factory for fifteen long years. He was delighted when the factory was ready for business and spent several weeks helping with the first glass batches melted in the new plant.

John Degenhart's Crystal Art Glass Company products from 1947 until his death May 14, 1964, were mostly in pressed glass—in many cases reproductions of very old molds. The molds for the Crystal Art Glass Company were made or purchased as follows: one at Martins Ferry, Ohio; one at Wheeling, West Virginia; one at Lancaster, Ohio; the remainder at Botson Mold Shop, Cambridge, Ohio.

Of the twenty-four molds that John pressed regularly, four were door or furniture knobs and one was a kettle mold. Nineteen were owned outright, including antique molds and copies of antiques: (1) bird in nest; (2) turkey (top on dish base); (3) hearts (toothpick); (4) Puss in Boots; (5) boots (high); (6) slipper (colonial bow); (7) lamb (top on dish); (8) hand (small outstretched palm); (9) elephant head (toothpick); (10) basket (toothpick); (11) shoe skate; (12) baby shoe; (13) bird with cherry (salt dip); (14) bird salt and pepper (with tops); (15) bird (toothpick); (16) tomahawk (the mold for this old tomahawk was given to John Degenhart by the president of the Cambridge Glass Company, Mr. Bennett); (17) covered heart jewel dish; (18) diamond, heart, spade, club; (19) sugar and cream. In October, 1964, Elizabeth Degenhart added a twentieth mold—a copy of an antique toothpick, which she called Colonial Toed.

Thirteen colors were mixed and pressed in the five cool-weather months annually in which John produced glass. The colors were amber, amethyst, amberina, sapphire blue, royal blue, milk blue, milk white, topaz, green, slag chocolate, persimmon, black, and crystal.

Of importance to paperweight collectors is the fact that Crystal Art Glass ran only an occasional crystal tank—usually twice a year, about the first of December and the middle of April. During these periods the entire annual output of John Degenhart paperweights was produced.

The most famous of the John Degenhart weights is the rose made in (1) red-and-white striped, (2) blue-and-white striped, (3) yellow, (4) white, (5) pale pink, and (6) powder blue. In one day (December 20, 1963), at the

Two Degenhart plaque weights. The Crystal Art Glass weight on the left was made in the early production days of the factory when John Degenhart pierced flowers at the corners of the opaque design plaque. The John weight was made in 1963. Flowers were no longer included at the corners of the plaque. Note the difference in lettering rendered by two different artists. (Photograph by George J. Melvin.)

Two Degenhart weights. A footed, one of a kind, ruby-red Degenhart rose with three green leaves. A Degenhart "window" weight: crystal enclosed a lily-type flower. The overlay color varied greatly from the palest blue to deep amethyst or opaque white. Usually a top and four side windows, or facets, were ground on these. (Photographs by George J. Melvin.)

John Degenhart at his bench or gaffer's chair. Note day's run of pressed ware chalked up on slate. (Photograph by George J. Melvin.)

age of seventy-nine, John Degenhart completed twenty-two roses—about one half footed, the remainder without a foot.

Other simpler paperweight designs made by John Degenhart in recent years at the rate of about forty a day include:

1. Butterfly—yellow or brown body and black or yellow spotted wings over multicolored base.
2. Four lilies, blue-over-white base.
3. Blue-white mottled, eight-part swirl or crimped base on center bubble.
4. A four-swirl crimped base with five bubble air traps—using red-and-white or green-and-white or blue-and-white colors intermixed where base was crimped. Placed in these weights were four perimeter bubbles and one center bubble.
5. Multicolored "double tree" with any date in the 1880's enclosed on crystal plate. These were made to order for individuals to commemorate important family anniversary dates. (At a recent antique fair one such weight was offered as "old" and priced at $42.)
6. A white-based, pink mushroom, red lily-type star flower.
7. The double tree (as John called it), resembling a six-petal, white flower growing from an eight-petal, white flower over a delicate, green base.
8. Multicolored base underlay with a white, opaque plate on which very interesting pictures, individuals' names, or verses were skillfully drawn by hand in vitrifiable colors, including designs such as Merry Christmas; Merry Christmas Sister; Happy Birthday; individual names (as ordered); covered bridge in color or black; Home Sweet Home (showing a log cabin).

Individualized weights were made to order by the Degenharts for many persons of note: Governor Orville Faubus; Colonel Robert Guggenheim; Texas Congressman, Albert Thomas; Postmaster General Day. Charles Degenhart prepared plates for the earlier individualized weights. He had considerable skill as an artist and did very intricate lettering and ornamentation on these plates. A very small, opaque white plate was frequently lettered with a name or an advertisement and encased as described above to form a $1\frac{7}{8}$-inch ball with a short neck. These balls were used as gearshift knobs on the floor shift in earlier automobiles. They were considered a deluxe accessory.

Bill Degenhart makes a star flower weight. (Photograph by George J. Melvin.)

Also made at the Crystal Art Glass Company were candle holders, lamp parts, bookends, doorstops, ring holders, and bottles with paperweight-type designs included in the form.

On Easter morning, 1964, the tank at the Crystal Art Glass Company burst, spilling the molten glass over most of the factory floor. Fortunately, the hot glass did not set the factory on fire. Four weeks of "working weather" were lost to the factory while the new furnace pot was fabricated and set in place. The factory had been in production again only two and one-half weeks when on May 14 John Degenhart died in his sleep.

With John Degenhart's passing, one of the most colorful paperweight manufacturers of recent years was lost to America. John was considered by his colleagues to be the very last active member of the "old school" of glassworkers.

Mrs. Elizabeth Degenhart and the five workers employed by the Crystal Art Glass Company are carrying on the work of novelty ware pressing. A nephew, William Degenhart, tried his hand at paperweights in September, 1964, with considerable success.

Bill Degenhart is a son of Charles and Pearl Moreland Degenhart. He was born on September 22, 1912, and was reared in Cambridge, Ohio. Early experience in glass manufacture was gained at the Cambridge Glass Company, where he assisted both his father Charles, and his uncle, John, in the making of weights.

Bill's first weights made at the Crystal Art Glass factory will always be easily identified, even though not signed. A slight error in compounding the ingredients of the first crystal batch mixed under Mrs. Degenhart's direction resulted in metal of very pale blue color. They were made in double-tree, star-flower, three- and four-lily, and five-bubble designs.

In September, 1968, Mrs. Degenhart lost her gaffer, "Zack" Boyd, who died following a very brief illness. Once again Bill Degenhart is crafting name weights for Crystal Art Glass until such time as a new gaffer can be trained for this production. Rollin Braden of Cambridge, Ohio, has taken over Zack's work as gaffer.

Chapter 4

Carl Erickson
Bremen, Ohio

A craftsman famous for his colorful art glass crafted with the unique bubble-design paperweight base was Carl Erickson of Bremen, Ohio. No book on contemporary paperweights is complete without mention of Erickson's production of skillfully crafted decorative and table-glass pieces. Paperweights, as such, he made in lesser number.

Carl Erickson was born in Sweden, May 21, 1899. Both his father, Carl Oscar, and his grandfather were glass artisans employed in the famous glass center of Reijmyre, Sweden. Carl was a lad of seven when his family immigrated to the United States. Father Carl found employment at the Mount Washington Glass Company, which later became Pairpoint and still later Gunderson Glass Company. Son Carl started his career in glass when eleven years of age. In addition to his experience at Pairpoint, Carl was employed at the Libbey Glass Company in Toledo, Ohio. For eight and one-half years he was production manager at the Blenko Glass Company, Milton, West Virginia.

In 1943 Carl and his brother, Steve Erickson, purchased a defunct glass plant at Bremen, Ohio. Ten years later Carl bought out his brother's interest in this plant. In the operation of the business Carl was ably assisted by his wife, Maude Akers Erickson, a niece of the well-known Gunderson of New Bedford, Massachusetts. Mrs. Erickson supervised the glass shipping and financial management of the plant.

Note: The data on Carl Erickson is from an unpublished manuscript by Ramona and Franklin H. Knower, Columbus, Ohio.

Carl Erickson at his bench. (Photograph courtesy of Ramona Knower, Columbus, Ohio.)

Examples of Carl Erickson paperweights. (Photograph by George J. Melvin.)

Some of the paperweights made by Carl Erickson include a design of three lilies in green or amethyst, a crystal weight embellished only by a series of very minute bubbles within the crystal, and a weight made with a bubble-pierced color core cased in crystal.

During the years of his active production, Carl Erickson was commissioned to duplicate many pieces of historically famous glass. Commissions included the duplication of complex glass fixtures found in old-fashioned laboratories for the Smithsonian Institution, Washington, D. C. Other pieces were duplicated for Old Sturbridge Village, Massachusetts; the Metropolitan

Examples of Carl Erickson paperweights. *Left:* The three green lilies with yellow-orange center, 3 inches diameter by 3 inches high. *Center:* Crystal bubble weight, $3\frac{3}{4}$ inches diameter by $2\frac{3}{4}$ inches high. *Right:* Amethyst bubble weight, $2\frac{1}{2}$ inches diameter by $2\frac{1}{2}$ inches high. (From the collection of Ramona Knower, Columbus, Ohio. Photograph by George J. Melvin.)

Museum of Art, New York, New York; the Corning Museum of Glass, Corning, New York; and the Ohio Historical Museum, Columbus, Ohio.

Examples of Erickson's art glass have been selected for display at many centers. At the Museum of Art, New York, his work won the Modern Design Award. A special display was circulated throughout European countries. Erickson was accorded the honor of blowing the first piece of glass from the furnaces in the reconstructed Jamestown Commemorative Glass Plant at Jamestown, Virginia, in 1957.

Colognes, candlesticks, compotes, bottles, vases, etc., most of them including the bubble-design paperweight base, were widely marketed from fine stores in the United States, Canada, and South and Central America. Erickson products gain constantly in appreciative acceptance and in demand by discriminating collectors of glass.

The many friends of Carl Erickson were saddened to learn of his death on February 6, 1966.

Carl Erickson art glass pieces. Note the bubble-design paperweight base on each piece. (Photographs courtesy of Franklin Knower, Columbus, Ohio.)

Chapter 5

Peter Gentile

John and Gertrude Gentile

Star City, West Virginia

Peter Gentile, born October 21, 1884, at Naples, Italy, was orphaned at thirteen years of age. To provide for his life necessities, he sought work in the glass factories of the area. Peter was undoubtedly an apt student for he is said to have been a glassblower at age seventeen.

About ten years later he immigrated to the United States. It is believed that his first American employment was at the Fry Glass Factory at Rochester, Pennsylvania, in 1911.

Peter Gentile's training in Italy stood him in good stead. He evidently learned many of the arts and skills of other craftsmen in the Italian factories and adapted himself well to the change to American factories. During the period of his employment in Rochester, together with another immigrant from France or Belgium, he made the famous Old Glory paperweight, to be described in detail later.

Following the closing of the Fry factory and with the removal of his good friend and boss, Joseph Haden, to Morgantown, West Virginia, in the early twenties, Peter Gentile was easily persuaded to join the Morgantown Glass Works. This factory was known as the Old Economy and now is called the Morgantown Glassware Guild, Incorporated. Peter brought many of his glass tools, molds, and dies with him to Morgantown.

To Peter and his first wife, whose maiden name was Charlotte Picone, were born five children—Rose, Mary, Helen, Frank, and Andrew. Both the mother and Andrew died in 1918 as a result of the disastrous "flu" epidemic.

John R. Gentile finishes one of his popular motto weights. (Photograph by George J. Melvin.)

In 1920 Anna Esposito of Naples, for whom the widower Peter Gentile sent, sailed to the United States and came to Rochester, Pennsylvania, to marry Peter Gentile. To this union were born Joseph, John, and Virginia. The work of Peter Gentile the father, and John Gentile his son, born on February 12, 1923, will be noted here.

Peter Gentile's quarter century in Morgantown glass factories must have been happy years. Besides the regular production turned out for his employer as a glass gaffer, Peter spent noon and evening hours after work experimenting, designing, and blowing glass in a manner much like that of the Italians in factories of his early training.

As Peter's sons grew up, three—Frankie, John, and Joe—joined him in off-hours or evening hours, three nights a week, in the manufacture of glass paperweights at the Guild factory. This quartet must have been a smoothly operating group, for as many as one hundred weights were made nightly. The demand for Peter's off-hour production was keen among the plant's buyers and jobbers, though in the beginning Peter made them as gifts for his friends. He is said to have given many of his handsome offhand pieces to friends when he would visit them.

By 1947 Peter Gentile built a small factory at 416 Industrial Avenue, Star City, West Virginia, along the bank of the Monongahela River in the heart of a glass manufacturing area of West Virginia.

Peter Gentile weights made prior to 1950. *Left:* Blue cane formed in spiral around blue center pointed bubble, 3 inches diameter by 3 inches high. *Right:* Orange, yellow, and pale green canes form a delicate spiral around large center bubble, 3 inches diameter by 3¼ inches high. (Photograph by George J. Melvin.)

John Gentile, the very young son of Peter and Anna Gentile, was introduced to paperweights at a very early age. The weight in John's hands encloses a photograph of Peter Gentile's first wife. A similar weight was cemented into her grave marker—a custom widely practiced in earlier days of paperweight manufacture in the United States. (Photograph courtesy of John Gentile.)

For a very short time in the early period of the Gentile Glass Company, John J. Funfrock, a mold maker, was associated with Peter Gentile, a craftsman. The company was known as G. & F. Glass Company, with Peter furnishing the craftsmanship and John managing the patents and accounts and designing molds. The patent designs used today in the Gentile glass factory production weights, namely, the butterfly with flower and the flying goose, were patented to John J. Funfrock in March, 1948. However, this partnership proved unsatisfactory, and Peter Gentile bought out Mr. Funfrock's interest.

Upon John Gentile's return in 1946 from service with the United States Army in World War II, he returned to glasswork, this time for his father. Previous experience had been gained in glasswork at the Guild, where he had advanced from carry-in boy to bit-boy before leaving for Army duty. John started his career in glass manufacture following graduation from Morgantown High School. He gained much experience while working with his father in the after-hours weight production at the Guild.

The versatility of Peter Gentile, craftsman, is apparent in the many examples retained by the family. A subtle fusion of blown and offhand work is found in many pieces. The favorite creations of which examples remain are:

1. Creams and sugars—striped blue or red or green over bubbled crystal.
2. Vases of all descriptions—usually with four or five feet crimped to

Peter Gentile weights. (1) Three pink mottled lilies out of white veil, $3\frac{1}{8}$ inches diameter. (2) Pale purple and white butterfly with silver flower over spaced bubbles, $3\frac{1}{4}$ inches diameter. (3) White flying goose with orange head over spaced bubbles, $3\frac{1}{4}$ inches diameter. (4) White and yellow butterfly, cane body with red and white flower over spaced bubbles, $3\frac{1}{4}$ inches diameter. (All from the collection at the John Nelson Bergstrom Art Center, Neenah, Wisconsin.)

resemble leaves (referred to by Peter as Dago feet), applied fluted tops, made in a large color range, but frequently red-and-blue striped overlay on white opal base.

3. Baskets—lighter glass bodies with dark green or blue feet and handle. Tops have a petticoat crimp and are finished with an encircling thread of glass.
4. Long swords—with crystal over orange, green, yellow, or crystal with multicolored handle.
5. Short swords—all crystal.
6. Canes—twisted crystal over one- or two-color interior threads.
7. Jam jars with tops—multicolored opal glass.
8. Lamps—blown and paperweight types.
9. Ivy bowls—blown with applied feet.
10. Fly catchers.
11. Wine pipe.
12. Paperweights—all descriptions, favorite colors yellow, orange, green, and red, white, and blue, including swirls, roses, and designs made from dies.
13. Spiral wig stands.

Peter Gentile's deep desire to express pride in his new country is apparent in the viewing of his many beautiful pieces of blown and offhand glass. A great majority of these are red-and-blue striped on opal-white backgrounds with blue trim. Orange, black, and green glass articles are to be found, too, indicating Peter's liking for various brilliant color combinations.

Gentile Paperweights

Old Glory is reputed to be the most famous Gentile paperweight. It has been made since before 1920 in a succession of three forms.

In the days when Peter Gentile was working in Rochester, Pennsylvania, he was assisted in the Old Glory weight manufacture by one whom he, in broken English, called Frenchie. Neither the name nor native country of this immigrant coworker is known for sure, but it is known that the two craftsmen combined to manufacture very unusual flag paperweights in red, white, and blue, using fine powdered glass for all parts of the flag setup, which was encased over a white base.

Gentile weights. *Left:* A Peter Gentile flying bird. *Center:* A Peter Gentile Old Glory. *Right:* A John Gentile flying bird, faceted. (Photograph by George J. Melvin.)

John Gentile snake weights and a hand cooler, showing the use of combined lamp- and pot-glass skills. (Photograph by George J. Melvin.)

John Gentile weights. *Left:* A rose. *Center:* A faceted millefiori. *Right:* A faceted rose. (Photograph by George J. Melvin.)

After Peter Gentile moved to Morgantown, West Virginia, weights of this same design were made with opaque red-and-white cane stripes and a blue ground-glass field in which thirteen stars appeared. These were made only until 1950, when the supply of glass rods imported from France could no longer be secured.

Since 1950 John Gentile has manufactured the Old Glory, using much the same process as his father except that the red canes are now transparent.

John Gentile weights: Old Glory, Butterfly, and miniature designs. (Photograph by George J. Melvin.)

Examples of Gertrude Gentile's craftsmanship. (Photograph by George J. Melvin.)

The cohesion factor of these canes has proved troublesome in recent manufacture. The 1964 faceted model is a true masterpiece.

The Old Glory design is most interesting in that it duplicates almost exactly the flag printed in the corner of the first official map of the United States of America, 1783.

As to the origin of the name Old Glory, a fine account is found in *The American Story Recorded in Glass* by Tracy Marsh.

John Gentile was delighted, during a visit to the Smithsonian Institution in Washington, D. C., to see displayed a very early flag of the United States designed almost precisely like the paperweight he has made so frequently.

The collector of glass is always rewarded by proof from a factory catalogue of the authenticity of any piece he may have. In the case of small glass factories, even today, very few catalogues are published. The Gentile Glass Company has three loose-leaf sheets showing pictures of part of their commercial production of forty-eight sizes and designs of paperweights.

Because Peter Gentile never saw fit to mark any of his blown, offhand, or paperweight production, one can verify the source only by actual identification by John Gentile. Earlier John did little to identify his work, having signed about six weights prior to 1963. Now he is putting a G or a J G in some weights he feels are collectors' items.

Some of the more skillfully produced paperweights made by the Gentiles included the footed, white-tipped, fourteen-petal rose in red, green, yellow, white, pink, light blue, and lavender, plus the many millefiori designs, the sulphides, and goldstone weights, loops, spirals, etc.

Both Peter and John Gentile learned a portion of their rose weight making from Winfield Rutter, a native of Millville, New Jersey, who as a young boy worked with Ralph Barber from 1905 to 1912. Rutter spent about a week at the Gentile factory in 1948 and showed the Gentile craftsmen how to make roses because he did not want the art to die out. He took a Millville rose crimp along.

Much can be said in praise of the Gentile weights. The popular swirl patterns made in delicate pink, red, orange, white, turquoise, pale blue, dark blue, and in some cases three different-colored canes, have been compared to the work done by the old Pairpoint Glass Factory at New Bedford, Massachusetts.

A group of Gentile dies for flower, motto, Masonic,
Eastern Star, Chase Manhattan Bank, and the well-
known butterfly with flower and bird designs.
(Photograph by George J. Melvin.)

Crimps used to create rose weights. (1) Hand crimp.
(2) Foot crimp—in other words, the pontil with gather
was shoved down onto this crimp held fast by craftsman's feet. (Photograph by the author.)

Gentile production weights. *Top row:* Motto weights. *Middle row:* Fruit, fraternal, and flower weights. *Bottom row:* Flower candle holders and weights. (Photograph by H. W. Ellis, loaned through the courtesy of John R. Gentile.)

The small-sized Gentile footed rose weight was designed somewhat as those made by Ralph Barber (1905–1912) at Whitall, Tatum and Company at Millville, New Jersey, or by Emil J. Larson of Vineland, New Jersey, who made large rose weights before retiring to live in Florida in 1947. Larson's ruby-red, pink, white, and yellow roses with three or four green leaves were made in a very limited number. The Barber roses ranged in red shades from deep red to a delicate pink; they were also made in milk white and yellow encased in a very clear glass. All the above were usually footed weights.

The more common Gentile weight designs that are sold to jobbers and gift shops throughout the United States and Canada today have designs of yesteryear including mottoes—"Remember Father and Mother," "Home Sweet Home," "God Bless Our Home," "Don't Forget Mother," "Friendship," "From a Friend," "Thinque of Me," "A Friend's Gift," and "Relax My Darling"—and the Eastern Star, Shrine emblem, and Masonic emblem.

Many of these Gentile motto dies were first used by Peter Gentile at the Fry Factory at Rochester, Pennsylvania.

Dies which John uses but which are another's property are some of the old Albert Graeser dies, including "Merry Christmas and Happy New Year," "Good Luck," the Masonic emblem, I.O.O.F., and "Atlantic City, New Jersey."

Other interesting weights by Peter and John Gentile include Old Glory, the flying goose, the butterfly with flower (the last two patented to John Funfrock in 1948), and the butterfly—of which there are five different variations.

The more common five flowers with center bubbles were sometimes made with a crystal bubble base, sometimes with a multicolored base. The

Examples of Gentile bubble and swirl weights, ashtrays, and candle and pencil holders. (Photograph by H. W. Ellis, loaned through the courtesy of John R. Gentile.)

flowers, which look like exploding fireworks, may be almost any color—blue, green, or yellow with white particles.

Identification of weights is all the more difficult because scarcely any are marked. Only continued study upon the part of the collector and actual conversation and comparison with the manufacturer can determine the exact origin of Gentile weights.

Both John Gentile and John Degenhart have had the experience of seeing pictures of their weights reproduced in books and magazines attributed to other artisans. At antique fairs both Degenhart and Gentile weights, made only four to six weeks prior to the sales, were being shown as old weights with prices ranging from $18 to $175. It is practices like these that make the artisans believe that contemporary weights should be identified for what they are and sold for prices comparable with present-day market value.

Almost countless Gentile weights have been made to order for large industries, associations, fraternal organizations, and for centennial and commemorative occasions. In some cases only a few have been made, while in others, up to five thousand or more were made.

The following is a list of some of the commercial production weights made to order by the Gentile factory; if quantity is known, it is indicated:

1. Commemorative: 1950, "Remember the Maine"—white letters and ship over blue background (using an old die), 50; 1962, Indiana County, Pennsylvania Fair, 6; 1956, A.D.S.A. University of Connecticut, Storrs, Connecticut, 75; 1960, McMinnville, Tennessee Sesquicentennial, 1,000; 1963, West Virginia Centennial, blue base, gold lettering, 3,500; 1961–1965, Civil War Centennial 1861–1865, blue lettering over white base, 24.

2. Lodge and Fraternal Organizations and Service Groups: Odd Fellows, Masonic, Eastern Star, Shrine, One Star (made for an Army General), 3; Olean New York Masonic Lodge; B.P.O.E. (lodge) #1772, Florida; West Virginia Mountain Lair of West Virginia University; Connellsville King Solomon's Lodge, 100; DePaul Praetorians and Coat of Arms (considered by John Gentile to be the most attractive commercial weight); Kappa Delta (green and white). In 1964, Walter Hrolenok took out a patent on weight designs which John Gentile will manufacture for eleven American

universities and colleges with their respective school colors. These will be limited to five hundred or one thousand per school year.

3. Organizations (a partial listing): Glass Bottle Blowers Association; Chico Dairy (milk-can shape in center); Brookville Glove Company (glove form in center); Orange Crush ("Your Guarantee of Quality"); Stewart and Grayson Coal Company; Barrett Cadillac Incorporated, Youngstown, Ohio; Three Termites; Rx Emblem (four dies); Straders of Pittsburgh; Chase Ribbon; Chase Cannon Prize; Charles M. Henry Printing Company, Pittsburgh; Tygart Valley; Smith Glass Company, Philadelphia; The Dallas *Times-Herald*; The 4 Wheels Incorporated Better Used Cars; Chase Manhattan Bank (two designs, 100 first, 114 second); Coca Cola; There's a Ford in Your Future; Cast by Findlay (for Findlay Clay Refractory, two designs); Blue Goose (for American Fruit Growers); Nationwide Insurance (four different designs); Star City Glass Company.

4. Parks, Gift Shops, Resorts: Cool Springs Park, West Virginia; Penn Alps, Grantsville, Maryland; SEA Antiques, Funkstown, Maryland; Coney Island, New York; Atlantic City, New Jersey; Nantucket Island; Pittsburgh, Pennsylvania; New Bedford, Massachusetts; a weight in blue and gold showing a large whale made in 1964 for sale at the New York World's Fair.

Occasionally John Gentile prepared a crystal name or date plate to be encased in a weight as a personal weight for collectors. Four were made with millefiori backgrounds; others were made with names in yellow, white, or black.

At a recent antique fair one of John Gentile's weights with a multicolored base and a clear glass plate bearing the date 1891 was offered for sale at twenty-two dollars. This was not an effort on the part of John Gentile to deceive a buyer, but rather was ordered by a private individual who later sold it to an antique dealer.

The most recent John Gentile weights, frequently incorrectly attributed to his father, are the George and Martha Washington weights. Delicately tinted portraits applied to white opaque plates are encased over multicolored red, white, and blue base colors. These John has been making since 1959 and now is dating and signing. The portrait of the late President John F. Kennedy, encased in crystal in a similar manner, is a very popular weight on the present-day market. Many of these weights are signed with an initial G and 1963 on the underside of the opaque white plate.

Other products of this factory include candle holders with a paperweight-type base, ring holders, ashtrays, lamps, and doorstops.

Other Work at Gentiles

As in the case of many small industries, all the production is not in one field. For economic reasons the Gentile Glass Company has a growing business in glass cutting by means of wheel grinding. Designs are cut very skillfully by James Hamilton, a stepson of John Gentile. The two divisions of glasswork—the manufacture of commercial designs in paperweights and the wheel decora-

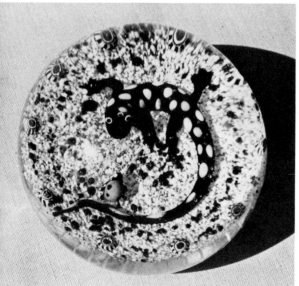

Lizards encased with flower or ladybug setups against jaspered grounds combine the skills of Henry C. Johnson and John Gentile. These magnum-size weights created since 1968 contain the signatures of both artists. Spaced millefiori pieces appear in many weights at the perimeter of the ground. (Photographs by the author.)

Gertrude Gentile, wife of John Gentile, is the only contemporary woman paperweight maker known to the author. (Photograph by George J. Melvin.)

tion of glass blanks produced at other factories—leave little time for experimentation with glass weight designs. When John Gentile does have time, he will try to make interesting millefiori paperweights. This takes the cooperation of his wife Gertrude, who usually does the setup—a preparation of carefully placed glass canes that may require one hour's work before the weight can be made by John.

Gertrude Gentile acts as carry-in girl for her husband, carrying the completed paperweights to the kiln for annealing. In late 1963 she became interested in making paperweights—a pursuit she is following at the rate of one paperweight daily with constantly improving dexterity.

By the summer of 1964 Gertrude Gentile's weights were selling from their display room on an equal basis of appeal with those of her husband. Gertrude Gentile is the only contemporary woman weight maker known to the author. As John says, "I have offered to teach many to make weights.

Only one pupil has truly mastered the ability to make beautiful weights. That one pupil is my wife."

In October, 1964, John Gentile made a series of his famous butterfly, George and Martha Washington, cane, and millefiori-design weights. These were all cut with punties and offered a new, very desirable line of Gentile weights to the contemporary collector. These are signed J.R.G. or Gentile. In the case of the Washington weights, a date, 1959, is inserted. This is the date John first succeeded in making these weights, not the date of manufacturing. The earliest Washington designs by Gentile were neither dated, signed, nor faceted.

Recent items crafted by John Gentile are a series (very limited) of miniature weights, mostly faceted, and a renewed production of the famous Gentile rose with four leaves. John proposes to make about two dozen roses annually for sale only to collectors. These are signed with the letter G.

In addition, some very interesting snake weights, spirals, and hand coolers are crafted by John. All are being made in a very limited number.

A skilled lamp craftsman, Henry C. Johnson of Ferry, Michigan, has created interesting snake, salamander, bug, beetle, flower, fish, and grape-cluster glass setups for enclosing by John Gentile in a fine new series of weight designs.

On September 6, 1969, Wapakoneta, Ohio, honored Astronaut Neil Armstrong in a great Homecoming Day. Two hundred citations, gifts, and

John Gentile's encasing of Johnson plain and striped snakes over jaspered grounds are attracting many collectors. (Photographs by the author.)

honors were bestowed upon him that day. Among these was one especially ordered by R. L. Yocum of the Neil Armstrong Homecoming Committee from John Gentile.

Upon receipt of the order for twelve paperweights John Gentile appealed to the C & C Mold Shop for quick service cutting two dies. One of these reads: "Moon Landing July 20, 1969." Centering the die is a moon with three craters visible and the command spaceship and landing module circling the moon. In stars on the edge are the initials J. G. to signify that the weight was crafted by John Gentile.

The second die has on the perimeter of the circle the names Armstrong, Aldrin, and Collins separated by stars which again contain the maker's initials. The interior of the die shows the Lunar Landing Module steps resting on the moon surface and a tiny astronaut standing beside the steps. These designs have been expertly crafted with a dark blue background color pieced by minute sparkly bubbles which could represent outer space and the planets of the universe. The designs are in a sharply contrasting white powdered glass. The weights are attractive, unique, and certainly collectors' items. They will be made in a limited number.

Recipients of the weights crafted for the September 6 event were President Richard M. Nixon; Astronauts Armstrong, Aldrin, and Collins; Dr. Billy Graham; Bob Hope; Governor James A. Rhodes of Ohio; the Honorable William M. McCullough, Member of Congress, 4th District, Ohio; John Herbert, Treasurer of the State of Ohio; Miss Easter Straker, WIMA-TV and radio personality; Fred Fisher; and Richard L. Yocum.

Mr. Gentile felt very honored to have been selected to design and make commemorative gifts for this occasion.

Chapter 6

O. C. Hamon
Fort Smith, Arkansas

Sometimes information about glass craftsmen eludes an author no matter what efforts have been made to get it. Such was the case with the Hamon family.

A farm boy, O. C. Hamon sought and secured employment in the Dunbar Flint Glass Corporation in September, 1916. His job was as a finishing boy (putting tops on glass lamp chimneys). Removing to Huntington, West Virginia, in 1922, Mr. Hamon worked for the American Thermos Bottle Company; a year later he went to McBride Glass Company, Anaheim, California; thence in 1924 to McBeth Glass Company at Marian, Indiana, for three years. Following a brief period of employment again at Anaheim, California, Mr. Hamon went next to Kerr-Hubbard Glass Company, Sand Springs, Oklahoma, in 1928; then back to his native state and Dunbar Flint Glass Company in 1930. Should you wonder why such a list of employments with dates is related, let me assure you that this moving about was quite common among the glassworkers of this era.

By 1932, Mr. Hamon started his own glass plant at Scott Depot, West Virginia, and operated under the firm name of Scott Depot Glass Company for fourteen years in West Virginia. In September, 1944, the location of the factory was changed—to Fort Smith, Arkansas, Box 152. This is really only the mailing address of today's Scott Depot Glass Company. The plant is located just three miles beyond the state line in Cedars, Oklahoma, off Highway 271.

Joe Hamon, son of O. C. Hamon, blocks a paperweight at his factory. (Photograph courtesy of Joe Hamon.)

Scott Depot Glass Company is best known for its novelty hand-drawn and hand-blown ware known as "Marigold Glass." These handcrafted pieces include the cornucopia, swan, morning glory, rose, and a variety of pitcher, decanter, and vase designs.

O. C. Hamon's son Joe has been operating his own plant in Durango, Colorado, since 1964, having learned his glass craftsmanship from age twelve, under the guidance of his father. Born in 1943, Joe Hamon has always "lived with" glass. He followed his father through the glass factory from the age of six. The Rocky Mountain Glass Company is located two miles north of Durango, on U.S. Route 550. Here Joe Hamon crafts the numerous "Marigold" pieces and some assorted designs of paperweights.

The O. C. Hamon's oldest daughter, Patricia Sue, married Donald L. Jones, who had been employed by Scott Depot Glass Company since he was sixteen years old. He was born in 1940. For two years now, Don Jones has operated his own plant, known as Pikes Peak Glass Manufacturing Company. It is located at 627 South Thirty-first Street, Colorado Springs, Colorado. As at the other two family plants, the "Marigold" hand-drawn and hand-blown pieces are crafted. Here they are known as "Pikes Peak Marigold." Twenty-one designs are crafted from Marigold and rainbow (multicolor) glass.

Most interesting to weight collectors is the fact that all three of these glasshouse owner-craftsmen can and do create paperweights. The rose is one of their designs.

Paperweights crafted at the Scott Depot Glass Company include roses in all white, red and white, and blue and white. Note that these are not footed. Three green leaves surround the base of the flower. (Photograph by Riggs Studio, Fort Smith, Arkansas.)

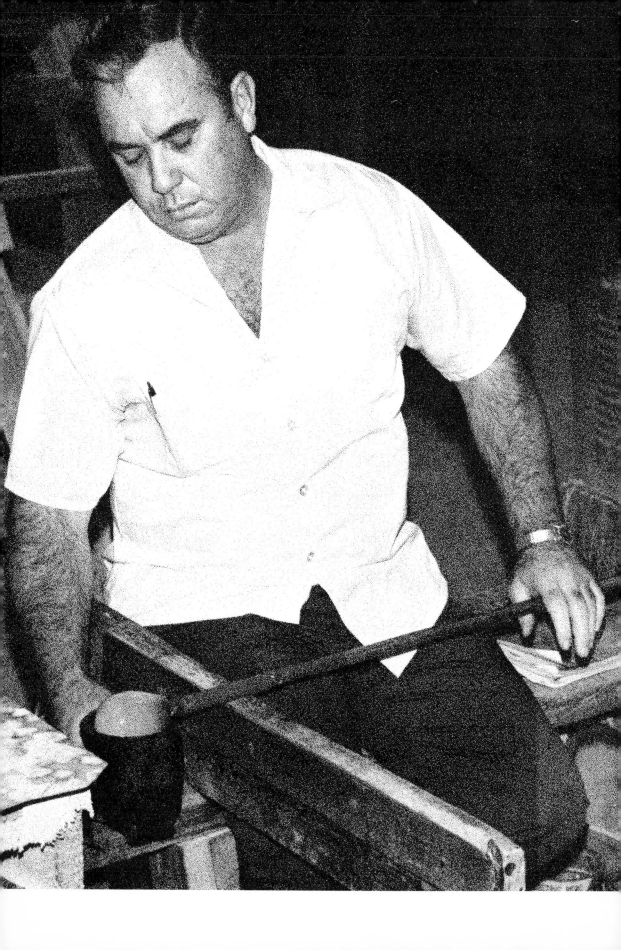

Chapter 7

Robert Hamon
Scott Depot, West Virginia

At Hamon Handcrafted Glass Incorporated of Scott Depot, West Virginia (a firm now associated with Kanawha Glass Company, Dunbar, West Virginia), Robert Hamon showed me several designs of paperweights crafted there, together with many colorful art-glass products. Mr. Hamon is endeavoring to build an art-glass line. Three lily-type flowers of white or rose or blue are frequently enclosed in a high-blocked weight. More intricately designed was a translucent yellow rose paperweight which Mr. Hamon says takes one hour to craft, using tin snips, block, and paddle. He explained that three petals of preheated marbles are placed in successive layers to make the rose weight with many reheatings and small encasing glass gathers. A final three leaves of green with brick-red centers (made of marbles) complete the color in these footed roses. Of course, the rose design must then be stuck up in reverse to add the foot. Mr. Hamon said these are made with marbles from Chinese checker sets. Some of the Hamon footed roses were made in red. None is made with a crimp. Tulips were also crafted at Hamon.

Robert Hamon, a nephew of O. C. Hamon, was born November 23, 1925. He has spent all of his spare time in the glass factory since his introduction to glass at the age of ten. He spent three years in the Naval Air Force in the Atlantic area. He has performed all the processes required for his glass production. Products of the Hamon factory found

Robert Hamon is plant manager for Kanawha Glass Company. (Photograph by the author.)

Howard Spurlack makes footed yellow rose paperweights. Each layer of petals is formed before a layer of crystal is added. (Photograph by the author.)

A translucent yellow rose footed paperweight made at Hamon Handcrafted Glass Company. Mr. Hamon says that the interesting green leaves with a brick-red stemlike center were made by melting marbles from a Chinese checker set. This rose is unlike any other I have seen. It requires an hour to craft a rose of this type as all the petals are added individually. (Photograph by the author.)

widely distributed in gift shops include paperweight vases, teapot ring-holder weights, cruets, vases, pitchers, ashtrays, swans, figurines, and candle-holders. Other designs include solid pear, apple-shaped, solid pepper, and tomato-shaped paperweights. Blown paperweights are made in pear and apple shapes.

Mr. Hamon employs about forty men in his glass factory, with usually three furnaces in operation, one reserved for experimental purposes. In one year, fifty-two colors of glass were made experimentally, using oxides and metals for colorants.

Paperweight products of the Hamon Handcrafted Glass Company include a green bubble design teapot, a paperweight-based vase in blue or green, and a regular size paperweight crafted with three flowers in pink or blue. (Photograph by the author.)

Chapter 8

Kent F. Ipsen
Northbrook, Illinois

A young man who has risen very rapidly in the art of contemporary glass crafting is Kent F. Ipsen. He is currently associate professor of art at the School of the Art Institute, Chicago, Illinois.

Kent was born January 4, 1933, in Milwaukee, Wisconsin, to Victor and Muriel Ipsen. His great-grandfather was a Danish potter. Other than this background of hand-skilled craftsmanship, Kent can claim no family glassworkers nor experience in industrial glass manufacturing on his own part.

His education beyond the public schools of Milwaukee includes a B.S. degree from the University of Wisconsin, Milwaukee, and M.S. and M.F.A. degrees from the University of Wisconsin at Madison. Following employment for a period of four years in all grades in Wisconsin public schools, Mr. Ipsen was selected as the instructor in ceramics and glassworking at Mankato (Minnesota) State College, a position which he held for three years prior to accepting a similar position at the Art Institute.

Ipsen creations have won much acclaim, with as high as three awards per show in both juried shows and invitational art fairs since he first submitted entries in 1962. Each year brings him additional art honors. Since 1967, he has been represented by one-man shows in galleries and museums of Wisconsin and Minnesota. His works are in demand for purchases for permanent collections by many colleges and universities of the mid-West.

Kent Ipsen experiments with hot glass to produce the unique paperweights he crafts today. (Photograph by Paul Herzfeldt, *Green Bay* [Wisconsin] *Press Gazette.*)

The interior of the neatly kept Ipsen glass shop shows a small batch furnace, glory hole, grinding and finishing wheels, furnace, and annealing oven. (Photographs by Anges Studios, Kenosha, Wisconsin.)

A limited number of doorstops and contemporary design paperweights are crafted each month by this artist. Mr. Ipsen estimates that his total monthly output is ten to fifteen with the greater portion of his production time given to the exploration of potential forms in the hot-glass medium. Encouraged by Harvey Littleton while a student at Madison, Ipsen has continued to create unique glass designs that appeal to many of today's collectors and art critics. His creations are constantly on the move for exhibition in art centers, museums, and colleges.

He is married to the former Shyla Fisher. The Ipsen family includes five young children.

Tools of the craftsman form a backdrop for a completed magnum-sized Ipsen weight. Note the unusually placed facets which enhance an interesting free-form design. (Photograph by Warline Studio, Hinsdale, Illinois.)

Chapter 9

John, Joseph
Frank, and Henry Kreutz
Riverhead, New York

Many of the beautiful offhand glass pieces crafted in glassworks today owe their beauty to the skill of craftsmen trained in Czechoslovakia or by Czech craftsmen who have passed along their skills to coworkers. The glass-buying public—were it possible for all to visit here—would thoroughly enjoy a visit to Riverhead, Long Island, New York, where Silverbrook Art Glass Works have a neatly kept factory. Here the buyer can see a piece made from start to finish by hand, by expertly skilled craftsmen.

The story of four Kreutz brothers and how they came to the United States is an interesting one. In 1928, John Kreutz, now seventy years of age, immigrated to Buenos Aires, Argentina, where he remained until 1958. In 1936, Joseph, now sixty-six and the only married brother, fearing for the safety of his wife and two sons, fled Czechoslovakia ahead of Hitler's 1938 seizure of the country. Brothers Frank, now sixty-one, and Henry, now fifty-six, joined Joseph in settling in Bolivia. Seven years later they went to Uruguay and then later to Argentina. On December 16, 1943, the three brothers, Joseph, Henry, and Frank, came to the United States. (There is one Kreutz brother still living in South America. Yet another brother, now seventy-three years of age, remains in their native Ledmoke Rovne, Czechoslovakia, to care for their ninety-five-year-old mother.)

Joseph and John Kreutz. Joseph is forming the head and trunk of an elephant. (Photograph by the author.)

Following employment in Tiffin, Ohio, and in Brooklyn, New York, glass factories, the brothers in 1946 established their own factory at 695 Flanders Road, Riverhead, New York. Only in 1958 did John join the trio. There were six boys and four girls in the family—the present four glass craftsmen of Riverhead representing the fifth generation of Kreutz skilled glass craftsmen. Since Joseph's two sons chose engineering as a career instead of glass, there will be no more glass artisans in this family.

Joseph, the chemist of the quartet, is the gaffer in the four-man shop. John is the paperweight craftsman, assisted by Henry. All the brothers are skillful and work together with a quiet ease and beauty of motion likened by some of their onlooking visitors to a ballet performance.

In their four-thousand-pound glass furnace each Friday is melted a

Silverbrook Art Glass Works produces many weights reminiscent of earlier Czechoslovakian production. John Kreutz created these four: two have frosted bases to show off the light yellow and red flowers. On the right is a millefiori rod weight with frosted mushroom underlay. (Photograph by the author.)

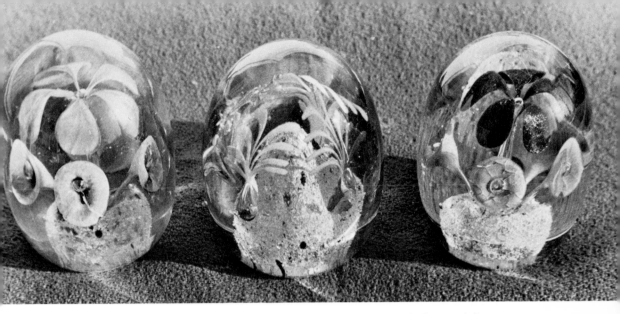

Silverbrook weights blocked in a high barrel shape include a pale pink five-petal flower centered over four small green morning-glory-type flowers which seem to grow from a brilliant white mushroom-type base. *Center:* Yellow, white, red, and blue glass canes centered to an air trap grow from a white base. *Right:* This weight has a brilliant green flower over four pale pink flowers centered to a white mushroom base. (Photograph by the author.)

"batch" of properly compounded ingredients to make crystal glass. After a fourteen-hour melting period, the 2700° F. crystal (metal) is cooled to about 1800° F. This is the usual "working temperature" used by offhand glass craftsmen. Monday through Thursday, September to June, the four Kreutz brothers combine their craftsmanship to create many offhand original glass creations.

No matter how many glassworks one has visited, the offhand glass process never fails to be fascinating. I was so intrigued by the skill of these four brothers that picture-taking was almost forgotten. The day I visited the plant, crystal elephants and lovely glass birds were being crafted.

The chubby elephant starts with a gather by Henry from the molten glass in the melting furnace. Henry marvers, then cools, this gather at the end of the pontil until Joseph is ready to shape and to impress pucella marks into the mass to indicate the elephant's legs. Frank appears with a smaller or bit gather which is fused to the body, "warmed-in" at the 2000° glory hole, and then a turned-up trunk is deftly pulled like taffy from the mass. Eyes are pierced and the mouth formed. Another molten gather is shorn off on each side of the head to form ears, and a tiny final bit gather attached at the rear of the body is pulled into a typical tail. After a final fire polishing and touchup, the elephant is cooled slightly under John's watchful eye, then struck from the pontil onto the floor of the annealing oven for a twenty-four-hour gradual cooling. This prevents fractures in cooled glass objects. In this time, the annealing temperature is reduced very gradually from 800° to room temperature.

In the showroom at Silverbrook are examples of approximately one hundred free-form offhand crystal glass items including a frog, whale, sea-horse, horse head, donkey, standing and sitting duck, rabbit, bird, snail, squirrel, deer head, turtle, pheasant—most of which could be used as paper-weights. Tableware includes cruets, bowls, plates, candy dishes, teardrop candleholders, ashtrays, captain's decanters, and the like. We did not mention the fish forms in the above list. On off-days the brothers do a great deal of fishing—then have been known to use the caught fish as models for crystal fish forms of great beauty.

Silverbrook products are widely distributed in the United States. In fact, my first sight of Silverbrook products was in a department store gift shop in New York City some years ago.

The Kreutz brothers, who speak very broken English, are quiet, pleas-ant gentlemen who go about their work in silent assurance that each is doing his part of the craftsmanship just as it should be done. They are assisted in sales and bookkeeping by two pleasant ladies, Edna Farruggia, their packer, and Maude Soltys, saleslady and secretary. These ladies showed me some small canes which had been twisted from hot crystal,

Silverbrook Art Glass creates many crystal forms which could be used as paperweights. The elephant enjoys great popularity. (Photograph by the author.)

made especially to sell to the many school children who annually visit Silverbrook.

Of course, my principal interest in visiting Silverbrook was to see paperweights made. While the brothers Joseph and Frank rested and took sips of cooling beer to relieve a constant battle against dehydration due to factory heat, brothers John and Henry demonstrated their skill in weight making.

John is indeed skillful! He is the first paperweight craftsman I have even seen using dampened newspaper to block the shape of his weight. John's designs are typically Czechoslovakian. He may use melted color to form five-petal flowers or he may apply four multicolor daubs which, when pierced with an ice pick to form an air trap or bubble center for each daub, resemble morning-glory flowers. The latter design he tops with a five-petal flower before making the final gather.

Recently John has been experimenting with creating his own glass rods which, when cut and set up, are used to form a simple millefiori design. Frequently John uses fine color rods or threads near the outside base of a weight design. When pulled with a tool at equal intervals, a resulting scallop of threads encircles the base of the weight.

I found John's designs colorful. They are entirely different in size, shape, color, and method of construction from those of all other United States glassworkers whom I have visited in my paperweight research. His weights are finished by wheel grinding to give a smooth, clear level base. They are identified by a sticker bearing initials S. G. surrounded in small-size type with the name Silverbrook Art Glass.

Chapter 10

Dominick Labino
Grand Rapids, Ohio

If I had a problem in glass manufacturing which needed to be solved, I would take it directly to Dominick Labino, a technical consultant and researcher for industrial glass for thirty-four years. Upon entering his glass workshop, one is immediately struck by the long rows of equipment. In addition to small block construction glass-melting furnaces and annealing ovens which he designs, one sees general machine-shop equipment, together with small melting pots for colored glasses and the usual tools of the glass craftsman.

In a second laboratory building of the Labino complex are interesting pieces of equipment for making tests of all descriptions on glass. Small boats of glass placed in one testing device indicate at what temperature the glass becomes cloudy or crystallized. In another machine can be made a 120-mile thread of minute-gauge glass fiber all from one ordinary-sized glass marble. Glass fiber is a subject close to Nick Labino's heart. He holds fifty-six patents on glass processes and compositions. Mr. Labino showed us two grades of fiberglass—one so soft that it looked like cotton, another much finer, which seemed to collapse when pressed between thumb and forefinger. A third implement in the experimental glass shop was a Geiger counter. Another device is used to measure fiber diameter by the rate of water flow. Still another device shown us was one for testing the softening point of various glasses.

Nick Labino uses a small wooden block to form a gather of glass at his bench. (Photograph by George J. Melvin.)

By far the most interesting testing equipment shown me was a type of polariscope. This shows the interiors of paperweights and other glass objects to indicate the presence of internal strain and stresses. The greater the rainbow spectrum within the object, the greater the stress. How I wish every paperweight craftsman and glass-manufacturing company had such a device! It would seem logical to me to make such a test before marketing paperweights and glass art objects and tableware, to remove any of poor quality that would injure their reputation if sold.

Mr. Labino, a cordial and friendly man, patiently explains his life's work, peering over his glasses as he talks to his fascinated listeners. He retired from Johns-Manville Fiber Glass, Inc., in 1965 where he was Vice President and Director of Research and Development. It is inaccurate to say that he retired. He really changed from industrial responsibilities to a life devoted completely to research and development of glass. This life, Mr. Labino believes, is possible only if the craftsman is a life-long student of glass and a constant researcher.

The glass colors Mr. Labino has created are like the finest jewels. He names the exact mineral or chemical ingredient used to achieve these rich colors. His knowledge of glass components, heating and annealing processes is so thorough that he needs not expect disappointing fractures and flaws because of guess work in batch mixing. His colors and the objects crafted from these color batches are an accurate fusion of research, experimentation, and craftsmanship with annealing and finishing.

Labino is an exploring craftsman. He has created "aerial sculpture" or "air sculpture" within the walls of many of his freehand-blown glass pieces. This is a process unique with Mr. Labino. He also created interesting glass sculptured pieces. For a man who began to work in glass as an art form only in 1963—a few years have brought forth an amazing production.

In his exhibition room are examples of Nick Labino's craftsmanship— no two alike. In glass cases are examples of a tremendous number of expertly compounded glass batches blown, tooled, and coaxed into forms of utility, grace, and harmonious beauty, some iridized, others decorated with applied threads of glass or other exterior decoration. Many are beautiful for their elegant simplicity of color and form.

Dominick Labino's paperweight vase with freehand morning glories enclosed. (Photograph by the author.)

When I inquired of Nick how many pieces he could make in a day, his answer, as I expected, was, "It depends upon the complexity of the craftsmanship. Some days I craft six or eight pieces, sometimes less." These, we observed, were carefully annealed in a fiberglass-lined electric oven or kiln where, by automatic controls, the temperature is reduced by minute stages until it reaches room temperature, and it is safe to open the kiln door.

For his paperweight production, Nick Labino uses no dies or crimps. He has beautiful tulips of iridescent lavender, a pale pink, yellow, or orange. Building three petals at a time, he creates a tulip of six or more petals—a design he has patented. Some of his paperweights are cased in crystal, others in pale blue or green glass.

A many-layered glass rod created by Labino (as the Italians created their millefiori rods) has succeeding layers of white, green, blue, until seven coats were applied and drawn into a rod. This was originally prepared as a display for the Corning Museum of Glass, to show how millefiori rods were created. However, a portion of this colorful rod was worked by Nick into five-petal flowers, which became the central design of paper-weights, cased in pale green glass.

An interesting paperweight of a sea monster, complete with bulging air-bubble eyes, was made of a spiralling rod of golden glass, a weight made without previously crafting the monster on a lamp. He swirled into life as the glass was worked. Flowers made of combined gathers of yellow, orange, and red; weights incorporating glass rods, bits, and air traps; paperweight vase forms—all these vie for the attention of the viewer. Many other designs were among the weights proudly displayed by Mrs. Labino in their glass-exhibition room.

Labino's work is more than contemporary; it is more than the creative hot-glass work being widely crafted today. Labino's work is glass crafts-manship researched, studied, crafted, tested, exhibited, and—by a discern-ing public—appreciated. One can readily understand this if he reads through a list of eighty-seven exhibitions where Labino's work was acclaimed. Of these, four were one-man shows. Twenty of the twenty-eight competitive

Paperweight vases are designs created using the paperweight technique. Note the matching morning-glory motif in vase and paperweight. (Photograph by the author.)

shows have awarded Labino honors. His works have been shown in thirty-five centers by invitation and are now in the permanent collections of twenty-seven museums, including the Corning Museum of Glass, the Toledo Museum of Art, the Cleveland Museum of Art, the Museum of Contemporary Crafts, the Pilkington Museum (England), and the National Museum (Netherlands). In 1968, the Board of Trustees of the Toledo Art Museum made Mr. Labino its first honorary curator of glass.

Dominick Labino was born December 4, 1910, in Clarion County, Pennsylvania. He studied at Allegheny Vocational High School and Carnegie Institute of Technology and later studied design at the School of Design of the Toledo Museum of Art.

His work has been reviewed frequently in current art and trade publications and he, in turn, has contributed much knowledge to glass researchers in his printed works which include: "The Egyptian Sand-Core Technique: A New Interpretation," *Journal of Glass Studies,* Corning, New York; The Corning Museum of Glass, VIII, 1966; *Visual Art in Glass,* in "Art Horizon Series," Dubuque, Iowa; Wm. C. Brown Company, Publishers, 1968; "Quartz Fiber Uses Broaden as Research Tempor Mounts," *The Journal of Commerce,* New York, Monday, Sept. 15, 1952; and "Standards of Testing Glass Fibers," *The Glass Industry,* June, 1963.

After visiting Mr. Labino's workshop, laboratory, and exhibition rooms, I believe that every collector who owns one of his unique glass creations—be it beautifully sculptured glass torso, a vase, bowl, or paperweight, or any other of a multitude of his fine works—should consider himself the owner of a treasure without price. His work is signed and dated.

Chapter 11

Emil Larson
Vineland, New Jersey

The dean of American glassworkers is Emil J. Larson, who retired from active work in 1949.

Emil Larson was born September 25, 1879, in Sweden, at the site of the oldest glass factory of that famous glass-producing country. Emil's father, Oxel, and mother, Marie, left Sweden for promised work in England, taking their family of eight with them. The family was increased by one member during the fourteen months' stay in England. Eventually there were ten children in the family.

Guaranteed passage to and a job in America, the Larson family arrived in New York when Emil was about eight or nine years old. While awaiting the train which was to take the family to White Mills, Pennsylvania, he and his sister strayed away and got lost. They saw a man selling apples and bought some. When they got back to the station, they couldn't find the family. In the meantime the train was called, and parents and family minus two embarked for White Mills. Can you imagine the predicament in which these two young immigrants found themselves when they returned to the railroad station? Penniless, in a foreign country, unable to speak the language, and no family to be found anyplace in the building, they spent the night in the station. The kindness shown Emil and his sister by understanding Americans at this railroad station was never forgotten. Fare for a later train to White Mills was sent by Christian Dorflinger. From this time on, Emil Larson has always referred to the United States as "God's Country." He says, "God bless it.

Mr. Emil Larson of Vineland, New Jersey. (Photograph by Maddock Photographers.)

This is the only country in which to live. She has the grandest flag in the world."

Emil Larson secured work in the glass factory of Christian Dorflinger at a very early age, continuing there for thirty years until the factory closed after World War I. Of Christian Dorflinger, Larson says, "He was the best boss a man could have."

On July 20, 1904, Emil Larson married Hattie Robertson of Brooklyn, New York. They have two sons living—a daughter is deceased. Of the sixty years of their marriage, fifteen were spent in White Mills, Pennsylvania, twenty-five in Vineland, New Jersey, and since retiring, sixteen years have been spent in Florida.

Emil Larson learned his glass-making skills by experience and by watching other skilled glassworkers. Charles Kaziun, who knows Mr. Larson well, says that Emil Larson was a most skilled worker—with superior ability in blowing glass, in copying any previously made glass masterpiece, and in forming rose-design paperweights. Larson knew well Ralph, George, and

Emil Larson's footed pale pink rose with three green leaves, in the collection of his friend, Arthur Gorham, Millville, New Jersey. (Photograph by George J. Melvin.)

Red Jersey rose with opaque
tips, twelve petals, and one
stamen, made by Emil Larson,
colleague of Ralph Barber.
(Photograph from the collection
of the John Nelson Bergstrom
Art Center at Neenah, Wisconsin.)

Harry Barber of Millville. "Ralph Barber was the only other man besides myself that made the large-size rose paperweight," says Larson. Ralph Barber made roses at Whitall, Tatum and Company, Millville, New Jersey. Other men working at this South Millville plant from 1890 to 1912 were Brays Shinn, Bert Wolverton, Moe Bailey, Harry Barber, John Reed, Tom Cossaboon, Art Hogan, Fred Vannaman, Alex Querns, Emil Stanger, Mike Stanger, Ever Smallwood, Marcus Kuntz, John Ruhlander, Michael Kane, Gabe Gland, and Cattie Hughes. This list of Whitall, Tatum and Company associates of Ralph Barber was furnished by Mr. Arthur Gorham, Millville, New Jersey, who clipped an article from the local paper.

Larson's experience in glassmaking included work at Dorflinger, White Mills, Pennsylvania; at Pairpoint, New Bedford, Massachusetts; at Durand Glass Works, Vineland, New Jersey; and in his own factory on West Chestnut Avenue in Vineland. No task in glass fabrication proved too difficult for him. He is credited with having originated the Durand overlay glass. His own backyard factory was torn down several years ago.

Larson says, "I made all my paperweights in my own factory. Replicas of the Jersey lily-pad antique ware were made in my own factory."

Larson proudly displays only a few examples of his fine handicraft. Most of his work he sold or gave away as he made it. At one time Mrs. Larson had a complete service of gold-ruby glass with which to set her dinner table. Among the pieces he keeps are a plate which won Larson a gold medallion prize at Philadelphia's Sesquicentennial exhibition; a ruby-red wineglass with a lion's head in the stem; an extremely thin blue butter dish made two days before he retired; a bottle in which a rose design appeared in the stopper but not in the bottom; an extraordinarily lovely glass vase, about fourteen inches high, which Larson said he made about seventy years ago.

Of his rose paperweights, for which he made his own brass crimp, he had only one—a beautiful ruby-red rose with white-tipped petals and four leaves. "The ruby I used I made myself using gold leaf," said Larson.

Larson's large-sized (magnum) paperweights made in red, white, and yellow with about sixteen petals and four green leaves are now quite hard to locate and command a high figure. Arthur Gorham of Millville, New Jersey, had the privilege of watching his friend Emil Larson finish up work on a rose weight. Few people were permitted this privilege. As Larson worked on a rose he would carry the work to the window, frequently thrusting it outside to examine it for needed improvements before finishing. Of every twenty-four roses made, Larson said he was lucky to get eight or ten good ones as so many broke in the annealing process. This breakage in Larson's opinion was not due to lack of care in annealing because he knew the temperature and how to control it.

In the years the Larsons have lived in retirement, many antique dealers and paperweight collectors have sought out their home in an effort to buy a Larson rose paperweight. In fact, Mrs. Larson wrote me that the (ruby) rose weight in the photograph of Mr. Larson at the beginning of this chapter, the last one in Mr. Larson's own possession, has been sold. Many collectors tried to buy it, so Mr. Larson set a price that he thought would be prohibitively high. Soon after he set the price, a collector willingly paid it.

Recently while talking with his close friend Arthur Gorham, Larson said, "I must have made a hundred good roses. Where did they all get to, do you suppose?"

Mr. Larson died January 20, 1970.

Chapter 12

Harvey K. Littleton
Verona, Wisconsin

A man who is doing a great amount of research and experimentation in glass processes today is Harvey K. Littleton of Verona, Wisconsin. Born in Corning, New York, June 22, 1922, Littleton had ample opportunity to observe glass manufacture during his youth and has always been interested in glass. However, he became interested in glass as an art form in 1958. Two years later he actively began research which placed him in the position of one of the leading revivalists of creative glass craftsmanship in the United States.

Prior to his interest in glass, Littleton gained fame as a potter, having exhibited and won awards in numerous national and international exhibitions. His work may be found in some twenty museum collections. He was a craftsman trustee of the American Craftsmen's Council (1961–1964).

Harvey Littleton is presently a professor in the Department of Art at the University of Wisconsin in Madison. He attained a Bachelor's degree from the University of Michigan and a Master of Fine Arts degree from Cranbrook Academy of Art, Bloomfield Hills, Michigan. In addition, he studied at Brighton School of Art, England. For a time he taught pottery at the Ann Arbor Potter's Guild, Michigan, and at the Toledo Museum of Art, before joining the staff of the University of Wisconsin in 1951.

More recently Littleton received grants from the University of Wisconsin and the Toledo Museum of Art for travel and research in glass. He

Harvey K. Littleton, experimental glass craftsman of Verona, Wisconsin. (Photograph courtesy of University of Wisconsin.)

was particularly inspired by the work of Jean Sala of Paris, who worked alone in hot glass from the twenties through the forties. Following his seminars in glass experimentation at the Toledo Museum in 1962, Littleton made a survey of glass schools in northern Europe.

Littleton's limited production must be accomplished in the brief time he is free from university teaching. He creates glass in a concrete-block building located on his farm near Verona, Wisconsin. In this workshop are produced glass vases, plates, bowls, and a limited number of paperweights. Most of this production is committed to exhibitions. A portion of Littleton's time is devoted to his teaching of classes in glassblowing at the Uni-

A blown weight made by Harvey K. Littleton in 1960. A free-form mushroom shape, not crystal, blue clear glass containing large bubble and dark canes from top of weight running to bottom. (Photograph from the collection of the John Nelson Bergstrom Art Center, Neenah, Wisconsin.)

versity, the first school to include such a course as one of the fields in which credit is given toward a Master of Fine Arts degree.

An example of his paperweight design may be viewed at the John Nelson Bergstrom Art Center and Museum, where an exhibit of Littleton's crafts was shown in the fall of 1963. More recent exhibits include those held at the Corning Glass Center, Corning, New York; Dubuque, Iowa; Little Gallery, Museum of Contemporary Crafts, New York; and Shop One, Rochester, New York. About seventy pieces constitute the exhibit—of these about one dozen are paperweights.

Weight collectors should be mindful of Littleton's six to eight graduate students who complete Master of Fine Arts work each year. These graduates are experimenting creatively in glass and may create paperweights of unique design in limited numbers. Named by Littleton as contemporary glass craftsmen are Marvin Lipofsky of Berkeley, California; Thomas Mac-Laughlin at Mt. Vernon, Iowa; Robert Fritz at San Jose, California; Dominick Labino in Grand Rapids, Ohio; Norman Schulman, Providence, Rhode Island; and Michael Boylan of West Burke, Vermont; Kent Ibsen teaching at the Art Institute of Chicago; and Fritz Dreisback at the Toledo Museum of Art. Work of some of these modern craftsmen was included in the last Toledo Glass National. This is a biennial competitive exhibition for contemporary glass artists organized in 1966 under the leadership of Otto Whittmann, director of the Toledo Museum of Art.

A very limited number of paperweights has been made by Littleton, as weights no longer hold a challenge or fascination for him. He uses a fresh approach for his glass design rather than the traditional.

Harvey K. Littleton was married in 1947. He and his wife Bess have four children.

It is important to the perpetuation of the glass craft in the United States that a man such as Littleton is creating and teaching others to create in hot glass. Too many crafts have been lost or have lain dormant for the lack of an interested, interpreting craftsman.

Chapter 13

Adolph "Otto" Macho
Vineland, New Jersey

A sturdy, squat man with straight, dark hair that belies his seventy-odd years is Adolph "Otto" Macho, Senior. Adolph Macho was born in Karolinka, Czechoslovakia, June 19, 1892. He trained in glassmaking in Moravia before immigrating to the United States in 1913. It was on Labor Day that he and Gus Hofbauer arrived in the United States on the same boat.

In New York City, Macho secured a union card. In an effort to secure work in the glass industry, Otto took a train to Chicago. Upon arrival in that city, he toured fifteen saloons, ordering the smallest beer served in each. Finally he caught the attention of a sympathetic bartender who acted as interpreter and inquired of the proprietor, for Otto, where their beer mugs were manufactured.

Macho was directed to the beer-distributing company, where again he asked where the beer mugs were made. He was given two addresses—one in Chicago Heights and one of a firm in Indiana. Seeking out the Chicago Heights address, Macho explained that he would like to make beer glasses. Escorted to a room filled with sample glass of all shapes and sizes, Otto was asked which ones he could make. Convinced that this young immigrant was a capable glass craftsman, Mr. Evan Kimble wrote a letter of introduction to Ralph Barber, manager of the Victor Durand factory known formerly as Vineland Flint Glass Company, Vineland, New Jersey.

Adolph Macho at his gaffer's bench in his home glass workshop. (Photograph by George J. Melvin.)

One week after arriving in Chicago, Otto Macho started his twenty-six-hour train trip back east to Vineland via Philadelphia. Arriving in Vineland, Otto walked along the railroad track for a mile, seeking out a building which by construction must be a glass factory. His letter of introduction presented, he was put to work as a gatherer in the shop of John and George Collini, fashioners of thermos-bottle glass fillers. Very soon Otto's skill won him the gaffer position (head man) in his own shop where he employed a Bohemian method of glass manufacture of chemical funnels. In this effort he was joined by his brother.

In 1916, Otto was tempted to join a factory known to the workers as Kimble Glass, adjacent to the Durand works in Vineland, where there were only 5 shops employed at the time. By 1921, an expanded Kimble laid off many shops of workers, but not Otto, who continued there until 1932.

When Victor Durand was killed in an automobile accident in 1931, Kimble Glass Company bought out the Durand works.

Otto Macho spent many of his years working between Kimble and Durand, crafting such items as funnels for chemicals, cylinders, and oil gauges of twenty-inch length to which brass tops and bottoms were added.

Otto clearly recalls working with Ralph Barber at Victor Durand's glass factory where Barber found employment after leaving Whithall, Tatum and Company. Otto declares that Barber did not make rose paperweights while at Durand, chiefly because the glass of the design and covering layers were not compatible, but made his famous weights before he went there. Ten roses attempted by Barber at Durand fractured, according to Otto. Another skilled craftsman, Emil Larson, came to work at the Durand factory in 1921, and in this same year Gus Hofbauer left Chicago to come to Vineland.

About forty-eight years ago (1922), Otto claims to have made two dozen rose paperweights. Of these he took two to the Boardwalk at Atlantic City, where he received $25 apiece. About two months later, he took another four roses to Atlantic City. This, he said, was a mistake, for the merchant, seeing four at a time, would offer only $10 each.

Otto has crafted roses ever since. In fact, in 1965, he made two dozen rose paperweights in his small glass shop located in the back of his home on R.D. 5, Vineland, New Jersey.

Macho has made many different weight designs. Shown are a yellow umbrellalike spatter design over turquoise ground, a footed thirteen-petal white rose with stamen cased in pale green glass and a three-flower pale blue morning glory over multicolor base cased with the brilliant crystal of the Durand Factory. (Photograph by the author.)

Otto's employment included periods at Vineland Art Glass from 1935 until World War II, when the factory burned down, a period of eight months in 1946 at Kessler Company, Bethpage, Long Island, New York, where he worked on lamp parts, and a period in 1946–47 at Wheaton Glass Company.

In the quiet of his small South Jersey shop, Otto fashions many off-hand products today. These are small and large spatter pitchers, vases, turtles (resembling the early South Jersey turtle paperweights), and a variety of designs of paperweights. He crafts weights with a butterfly, an umbrella-like spatter design, a three-flower, and a five-petal-flower design. He had only one rose to show when we talked with him, but he has made footed rose paperweights in a variety of colors. Paperweights, as such, he has crafted since his early days of employment at Victor Durand's factory in Vineland.

Otto's wife's name is Mary. They had three children, two sons and a daughter. The oldest son was a B-25 bomber pilot lost in action in World War II.

Note: To help clarify factory names of the period this story covers, I appealed to Mrs. Raymond Bassett, Director of the Wheaton Historical

Otto Macho discusses his morning-glory and rose paperweight designs. Note the Czechoslovakian photograph weight in the rear. (Photograph by George J. Melvin.)

Gus Hofbauer, a longtime friend and associate of Macho, crafted this three-blossom yellow and white morning-glory-type flower over apple green base color surrounded with seven light reddish orange tooled glass threads. (Photograph by the author.)

Association. She kindly sent me a photostated copy of an announcement card circulated in 1912 which reads:

KIMBLE-DURAND GLASS CO.

We beg to announce the consolidation on September 15th, 1912, of the interests of the Kimble Glass Company and the Vineland Flint Glass Works.

The new corporation will be known as the

KIMBLE-DURAND GLASS COMPANY,

with general office at Chicago

Factories at Chicago, Ill., Vineland, N.J., Millville, N.J.

KIMBLE GLASS CO.   VINELAND FLINT GLASS WORKS
E. E. Kimble, President   Victor Durand, Jr., Prop.

She further revealed that in 1968 two workers, Samuel Caralluzzo and Eugene Crabtree, made a few experimental glass paperweights at Wheaton Glass.

Chapter 14

Tom Mosser
Cambridge, Ohio

After several years spent in researching and collecting paperweights, it is always interesting to me to view a weight-filled salesroom or a personal collection of weights. The challenge is, How many can I correctly identify?

One day a trip to the Sickle Glass Shop at Bellaire, Ohio, proved most interesting for this reason. While I awaited completion of a grinding job, I looked over the weights that Mr. Sickle had for sale. I recognized Gentile, Degenhart, and St. Clair products, but was stumped by one group of paperweights. I asked, "Are these Cambridge weights?" thinking they might have been crafted at Mrs. Degenhart's factory. "Yes," was the reply, "those are made in Cambridge, Ohio, by Tom Mosser." Mr. Sickle then related quite a story about Tom and his factory.

Many months later I again heard of Tom Mosser. He visited John Gentile's factory and, for once, John had to admit that he didn't spot Tom Mosser as a glass craftsman when he stood watching John making paperweights.

Tom is a tall, pleasant fellow who looks much more like a professional athlete than he does a glass craftsman. Tom is a son of Orie and Jennie B. Mosser and was born in Cambridge, Ohio, on March 15, 1927.

Tom's father was a glass craftsman all of his working years—having worked at Marietta Glass Company and finally for more than fifty years at the Cambridge Glass Company. In fact, he was factory manager at Cambridge and received a gold watch in recognition of his long service

Tom Mosser of Variety Glass crafts a paperweight. (Photograph by George J. Melvin.)

there. A. J. Bennett was a long-time owner of the Cambridge Glass Company, and it was Bennett's son-in-law, Mr. Orme, who gave Mr. Mosser the fifty-year watch.

At age sixteen, Tom left school to go to work at the Cambridge Glass Company. He progressed from carry-in boy to warm-in, then gatherer for tableware and presser. Prior to the closing of the Cambridge works in 1957, Tom had worked up to assistant foreman.

A glassworker by the name of Mr. Wencek, a friend of Tom, had a sizeable chicken coop on his property in Cambridge. In this chicken coop the two former Cambridge Glass workers set up a small factory. Learning of the closing of A. H. Heisey factory at Newark, Ohio, they bought and trucked some of the Heisey tank blocks to their factory.

The heat generated from the rebuilt one-thousand-pound glass tank was so intense that the two workers could stand to work only between the hours of 5 and 8 A.M. They manufactured drug glassware for Miss Mitchell, also a former Cambridge Glass employee. On March 14, 1960, fire leveled the makeshift factory.

Tom Mosser designed these two weights, a multicolor center swirl surrounded by deep air traps and a blue glass weight with a crimped design. (Photograph by the author.)

Mosser and Wencek established a new firm with Miss Mitchell as a partner. The new company leased a tank and a lehr in the buildings of the former Cambridge Glass works. For one year, glass was turned out at the Cambridge plant.

Variety Glass, Incorporated, has been in operation for nine years. A former Cambridge street-car barn owned by the Ohio Power Company was purchased by Variety Glass and proved to be an adequate building for relocating the glass company. Then, early in 1966, Mr. Wencek retired. Tom and Miss Mitchell became sole owners. All went well until July, 1966, when this building was partially destroyed by fire. Only three outside walls remained standing.

While rebuilding the factory, Tom, undaunted by two fires, went to his own small plant in the Fairground addition and continued to manufacture glass. By October, 1966, the rebuilt plant was ready for occupancy. Today it furnishes employment for fourteen men, eight of whom are former Cambridge Glass employees.

From the Cambridge Glass Company, Variety Glass was able to secure many presses and a good lehr. The principal output of glassware is for chemical, laboratory supply, and physicians', druggists', and watchmakers' glassware. However, Tom Mosser markets from his own twenty-two molds some very colorful novelty salts, jam dishes, toothpick holders, ashtrays, boots, and slippers in a variety of interesting forms.

On weekend off-hours, Tom creates paperweights. Many have hand-painted designs, scenes, or nameplates (created by Ray Bichard, of Cambridge) enclosed in crystal. Mr. Bichard also paints plates for Mrs. Elizabeth Degenhart to enclose in her factory weights. To distinguish which factory cases the plates, Mr. Bichard places a "D" for Degenhart and an "M" for Mosser on the plate proper. Shrine and Masonic weights and some flower designs are created by Tom also at Variety Glass, Incorporated, 201 Foster Avenue, Cambridge, Ohio.

Chapter 15

Edward Rithner
Wellsburg, West Virginia

Six young men left Monthey, Switzerland, in the 1880's for Canada, where they hoped to find employment among the French-speaking population of Montreal. However, the employment they secured was short-lived. Thinking there would be greater employment possibilities elsewhere, the men decided to try their luck in the United States. Among these six young men were Emile Constantin, Louis Rithner, Henry Rithner, and Nicholas Kopp. The Rithners were natives of Switzerland, Henry having been born there in 1866. Nicholas Kopp traced his ancestors back two hundred years to the glassmakers of the Lorraine Forest of Alsace-Lorraine, whose skill was considered so secret that its practice was kept within the bounds of glassmaking families. This fine training and background in the skill of glass production was a tremendous help toward his finding employment in the United States.

Part of this group of immigrants came to Wheeling in 1888 where they found work in the glass plant of Hobbs, Brockunier and Leighton. While employed there, Nicholas Kopp met and married Frances Marschner, and Henry Rithner married a sister, Virginia Marschner. The parents of these two girls were both active members of the glass industry: the father, a native of Bohemia, having been an artist at Sandwich and the mother being actively engaged as chief decorator at Hobbs, Brockunier and Leighton.

To the Henry Rithners were born two sons: Edward, born January 10, 1890, in Wheeling, West Virginia, and Henry, born in 1896 at Coraopolis, Pennsylvania. As these sons matured, they too worked in the glass industry.

Edward Rithner with some of his dies. (Photograph by George J. Melvin.)

This same group of close friends left Wheeling in 1889 for the Fostoria Lamp and Shade Company at Fostoria, Ohio. Nicholas Kopp removed to Coraopolis, Pennsylvania, in 1896, where he started the Consolidated Lamp and Glass Company. Of course, his skilled workmen and friends followed him in this new adventure. At a later date Mr. Kopp went to Swissvale to the Pittsburgh Lamp and Brass Company, which is known today as the Kopp Glass Company.

While Henry Rithner, Sr., was employed at the Consolidated Lamp and Glass Company plant in Coraopolis, Pennsylvania, his son Edward recalls that he started his formal education as a first-grade student in the public schools. This schooling proved all the more difficult because he understood only the French language—as spoken in his home. All the time Ed attended school, he acted as assistant to his father in glass production during the after-school hours.

As an apprentice to his father, Ed recalls working in the backyard experimental glass shop affectionately known as the Shanty. Here much study of chemistry, coupled with constant experimentation by his father, resulted in such successful production as to evoke praise and commendation from contemporary glass craftsmen. Included among the many products made here were paperweights. These Ed was entrusted to hold on the pontil until they were sufficiently cooled to place in the annealing oven.

By the time Ed completed the eighth grade, formal schooling ended for him. The school of experience in glass manufacture proved to be interesting with an ever-changing setting. In quick succession, as was the case with most of the skilled glassmakers of that era, the family moved from plant to plant. They went to Fostoria, Ohio; Moundsville, West Virginia; Brilliant, Ohio; Martins Ferry, Ohio, ("Hasken"); the Wheeling Glass Letter Company, Wheeling, West Virginia; the West Virginia Bottle Factory, Lazearville; and finally Wellsburg.

On July 8, 1908, Henry Rithner, Sr., established a glass business at Lazearville, now part of Wellsburg, West Virginia, removing to Wellsburg, in 1911 when he bought the Riverside Glass Factory and formed the Crescent Glass Company with a Mr. Worthen as a partner. Wellsburg, formerly Charlestown, Virginia, is said to be the second oldest town on the Ohio River. The river earlier had proved to be an excellent trade route for glass shipped from Ohio River glasshouses to areas of the West and South. Many of the early glass factory names, now identified as Wheeling glass firms, had their beginning at Wellsburg, including Hobbs and Dalzell (now Erskine).

The Crescent Glass Company has enjoyed an excellent reputation especially for cranberry and ruby glass products, today manufacturing much signal and ecclesiastical ruby glass. In the sixty years of Crescent's existence, it has built a reputation unequaled in the industry for harmonious industrial relations.

At the Crescent Glass Company, Henry Rithner's sons, Ed and Henry, grew in the knowledge of glass production and plant management. Henry, Jr., has operated the plant since his father's death. Today the third generation Henry Rithner assists his father in guiding the destiny of this plant.

In 1939 at his father's death, Edward Rithner left Crescent to follow in the footsteps of his father in the production of original offhand glass creations. There is no doubt that previous knowledge and experience helped Ed in his venture, but as he explained, "I did assist my father and watch him make

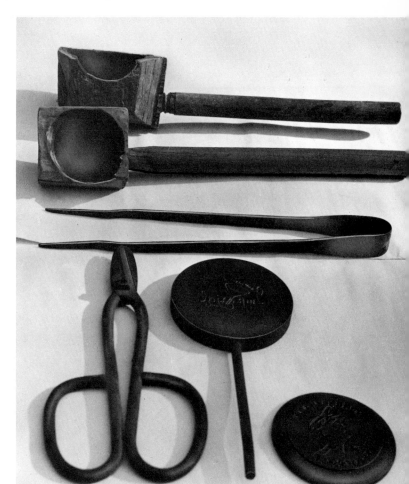

Paperweight blocks and tools used by Edward Rithner. (Photograph by George J. Melvin.)

Dies which Edward Rithner used in paperweight manufacture. (Photographs by the author.)

weights experimentally, but I never did make a weight myself under his guidance."

How did Ed Rithner happen to settle upon the manufacture of paperweights as a production item? Ed says, "I went to New York City and toured all the shopping area searching for some item short in supply." Back in Wellsburg again, Ed built a backyard shop complete with day tank, crucibles, and annealing oven. Here he worked skillfully until his retirement in 1951 to manufacture paperweights, ashtrays, scent bottles, cream and sugar sets, bookends, doorstops, and vases. He says, "I made just what I pleased, and the world will never know how much was turned out per day."

Ed's childhood training in grinding glass colorants for his father served as background experience for use of fine-ground glass in dies and color layouts for weight manufacture. Too, his early experience in testing glass batch maturity by placing the rod in a small crucible helped assure Ed's successful weight manufacture. All of the multitude of unusual weight designs were Ed's own ideas, very acceptable to the buying public as was proved with brisk sales in both New York's and Chicago's leading stores.

Some Rithner weights contain multistriped candy canes so real in appearance as to be almost "tasted" when viewed. These canes Ed designed and pulled himself by a very ingenious method.

Differing from other weight manufacturers, Ed Rithner chose to grind and chip unwanted breakoff glass away from the pontil base of his weights. This painstaking chipping left easily identifiable tool marks and an opaque or frosted appearance at the concave base of each weight. This area was frequently covered with a gold sticker before being shipped to the sales points. Ed recalls that he learned this method of weight finishing from his father.

This chipped finish is the most readily identifiable method of distinguishing Rithner weights, as no signature appears on any I have seen.

Colors in Rithner weights help distinguish them as Ed's work, too. The colors fall roughly into four classes:

1. Ruby-red flowers or designs over opaque white base colors. This ruby red was made with gold which cost thirty-five dollars per ounce. Only the ruby made with gold could withstand the intense heat required for paperweight construction.
2. Rose-pink fine-ground glass flowers edged with fine white ground glass, suspended over white base color.
3. Same as above only turquoise is used for the flowers.
4. Royal blue used in design forms combined with opaque white.

Of course, there are yellows, oranges, greens, and other colors used also, but not as frequently as those mentioned above.

The type of flower made by Ed, with Mary Rithner's assistance in the setup, is most beautiful and is easily distinguished. No other weight maker has achieved this type setup to my knowledge. The flower design may be in rose, turquoise, or royal blue, with the edge and under-color of each petal delicately etched in white. The flower may be a five-pointed star or a six- or eight-petal flower emerging from one center bubble. Usually the setup is enhanced by an opaque white base, or perhaps a mottled-blue and white or a ruby-red and white base is used.

A record of the various weight designs on display or mentioned by Ed as having been made by him include:

A. Motto or die designs (also called inscription weights)
  1. Merry Christmas. Letters appear within a wreath which has a twisted lighted candle at base of wreath design.
  2. Mother. Letters centered, top and bottom white flower sprays over red base.
  3. Home Sweet Home. Cabin with two doors, five windows, one tree on right of cabin, top of tree behind cabin at left. White path branching

two directions. White powdered-glass picket fence, blades of grass, and roof markings.

4. Hero-of-the-Philippines. A bust of the late General Douglas Mac-Arthur.

5. Messenger of Love. White bird in flight, carrying letter, over multi-colored base.

6. Messenger of Love. Bird in flight carrying envelope. Red bird over white lined base of thirty-six loops made by the crossing of extremely fine powdered-glass opaque white lines.

7. Think of Me. Two flowers on a single stem, all of white powdered glass, the motto also of white powdered glass over a multicolored base.

8. Imperial Glass Corporation. A piece of stemware in white powdered glass over a scalloped blue base with white line edge. The name *Imperial* is done in a script letter of white powdered glass.

9. Individuals' names. White letters, white flower spray below letters of name, bird in flight above name. (Ed made many name weights for

Edward Rithner weights: some of his many flower and butterfly designs. (Photographs by the author.)

Edward Rithner weights: Imperial Glass Corporation weight, candy cane, white bird, and flower weights. (Photograph by George J. Melvin.)

prominent individuals of the eastern United States. The weight included the individual's name, a white dove or bird, and if requested, the date—all showing plainly in white powdered glass over a multicolored glass-fragment base. Ed's finely designed inscription weights should not be confused with those of inferior quality made by persons attempting to copy his work.)

10. White cross of powdered white glass surrounded on left and right sides with white spray (powdered glass) over red base color.
11. White butterfly of powdered glass over a multicolored base.
12. Sixteen-white-petal flower with cobalt-blue center around single center bubble over white lined base of thirty-six loops.
13. Sixteen-narrow-petal, light-blue flower with white edge on every petal over white lined base of thirty-six loops resembling a doily.

Note: The very first Henry Rithner weights are said to have been mold designs, one commemorating the sinking of the Maine and the other glorifying Dewey—Hero of Manila.

B. Candy-cane weights
1. Broken canes of various colors (*vertically* striped) over a red base color.
2. Broken candy canes over white base color. These candy canes have *twisted* color striped of varying widths in red, turquoise, pink.
3. Red, white, and blue striped twisted canes centered to a large air-trap bubble to form a crown which shows plainly over opaque-white base color.

Edward Rithner weights: some of his many flower designs. (Photograph by the author.)

    4. Various colored canes radiating from center bubble to form a crown over a small center white opaque mushroom accented by mottled red-and-white base color. Four perimeter bubbles show in the red-and-white base color.

C. Flower weights
    1. Eight-petal white crocus-type flower over red-and-white mottled base.
    2. An eight-petal daisy-type flower, petal coloring resembling diamond-like bits over opaque-white base with four perimeter bubble air traps.
    3. Eight-petal flower, top surface of petals cream colored over turquoise under-petal color, red stamens.
    4. Nine-petal rose swirl flower over turquoise swirled base of nine divisions.
    5. Five-petal flower with large center bubble. Inside of petals red, under-coated with white, over a multicolored base. This is a footed weight, top shaped like a hand cooler.
    6. Four-petal, dark-red flower centered over a five-lined turquoise intermediate color arrangement (made with a die), which is pierced by four perimeter bubble air traps. Entire design over an opaque-white base.
    7. Five-pointed turquoise star, large center bubble over turquoise square, all the above edged in white. This weight has a cream base color, pierced by four perimeter bubble air traps.

8. Spherical weight containing three eight-petal flowers which face the circumference of the sphere. One flower is pink, one turquoise, one royal blue, all with bubble centers appearing over a multicolored base.

9. An eight-petal daisy-type flower. Each petal has a white center surrounded by royal blue, underlaid with white. The base is a leopard-spot arrangement of blue and white with four perimeter bubbles.

These examples of Ed Rithner's work are included to help collectors recognize his weights. Note the careful lettering in his HOME SWEET HOME, the delicately etched white edge on the five-petal flower, and the interesting butterflies of the other weights. (Photographs by the author.)

10. A star flower of five white petals with spots of red radiating from the center bubble. Three rose petals edged in white spread from six perimeter bubbles to form a chain around the weight accented by opaque-white base.

11. Eight-petal flower, turquoise with white edging, petals growing from a center bubble. Three turquoise petals edged in white grow from six perimeter bubbles. All of this color appears over an opaque-white base.

   Note: Similar weights were made with eight rose petals edged in white.

12. Eight-petal flower, yellow center, red-tipped petals edged in white growing from center bubble, over yellow-and-white base color in which there are four perimeter air traps.

13. Eight-petal flower made with ruby-red, white-edged petals centered with large bubble. Flower grows from mottled ruby-red and opaque-white base color which has four perimeter air traps.

D. Bottles
   1. Large bottles 7 inches high and 5 inches diameter. Made with lovely lily-type flower in stopper. Flower is made with one white, one turquoise, and one red petal, centered to a bubble. Base of bottle is very heavy glass in which layers of ruby-red, turquoise, and white are overlaid, pierced by four perimeter bubble air traps.
   2. Cologne bottles made with five-petal star flower in either turquoise or royal blue edged with white in stopper. Base of bottle is made with similar colors in layers pierced with four perimeter bubble air traps.

E. Other Rithner products
   1. Creams and sugars. Made with either blue and opaque-white mottled colors or rose and white delicately designed.
   2. Ashtrays.
   3. Cigarette holders.
   4. Bookends. Spheres designed similarly to weights, with eight-petal pink or turquoise flowers over matching mottled base colors. Spheres were one-quarter turned, then attached to either square or semicircular base of crystal glass.

There are certainly many more Rithner weight designs than have been mentioned here. Perhaps there are other miscellaneous Ed Rithner products I have not recorded. It is difficult when researching any weight maker to record accurately all the items attempted because many times only one or two weights of a kind exist. The majority of Ed Rithner's weights were sold in large cities of the United States by dealers who never disclosed the exact source of supply. Some Rithner weights were retailed from the show-room of the Imperial Glass Corporation, Bellaire, Ohio.

I believe it is proper to include in this chapter the few facts I have gained on the life of Emile Constantin, who came to Coraopolis, Pennsylvania before 1900. In July, 1967, I had the good fortune to visit Arnold Constantin (youngest son of Emile) and his wife, Grayce, in their home, where I saw many examples of his father's work.

Emile Constantin was born in April, 1860, and died in 1943. He made paperweights at night. Beginning in 1930, his wife Victorine helped by filling fire-clay dies with glass which had been pulverized with mortar and pestle. She used a paper funnel. As many as twenty-one weights per night were made by Constantin and placed in the lehr to anneal. However, many of the best weights he never saw again unless he returned very early to the factory the following day. From an interesting and accurate daily diary which Emile kept, he noted that two to seven of his paperweights were stolen each production night at Consolidated Lamp and Glass Company in Coraopolis, Pennsylvania.

Antique Fakes and Reproductions by Ruth Webb Lee shows two examples of Constantin's work.

Some of the finest of Emile's weights were given to his personal physician, Dr. E. M. Iland, and to a banker friend, Charles Ferguson. They are cased in the finest of crystal so clear it was referred to as X-ray glass by the famous batchmaster, Mr. Greenwald.

Chapter 16

Joseph, Edward, and Robert St. Clair

Elwood, Indiana

John St. Clair, Sr., immigrated to the United States from Alsace-Lorraine with his parents when he was twelve years old. His father, a glassmaker who first found employment in Crystal City, Missouri, removed to Elwood in 1890, when the Indiana gas boom also brought about an acceleration in glass factory building. Both father and son found work at the MacBeth-Evans Glass Company as lamp-chimney workers.

John B. St. Clair and Nellie Carroll of Elwood were married in 1903. To this union were born five boys and five girls. Of this family three boys are still actively engaged in the St. Clair factory: Joe, born February 18, 1909; Bertrand Edward, born July 21, 1912; and Robert, born May 18, 1919. John, the oldest son and the third generation John, worked with his father and brothers for a time before securing work in Anderson, Indiana. He died quite suddenly, and John B. St. Clair, Sr., the father, passed away December 28, 1958. Mrs. John St. Clair, Jr., is the secretary—office manager–saleslady of the St. Clair Glass Works.

The present-day St. Clair production is the result of the skilled workmanship of Joe, Ed, and Bob St. Clair and two helpers they have trained. There are no boys in the younger St. Clair generation to whom this skill can be passed. However, all three of Joe's attractive daughters show keen interest in glass manufacture and assist in it when possible.

The St. Clair Factory is located at 408 North Fifth Street, Elwood,

Ed St. Clair brings an unfinished weight to Joe's bench for blocking while Bob waits to pick up the finished weight to carry it to the fire-polish bench. Having fire-polished the pontil breakoff, Bob then places the weight in the annealing oven. (Photograph by George J. Melvin.)

Indiana. On June 4, 1964, a glass tank burst, spewing hot glass over the factory floor and resulting in a disastrous fire. The St. Clair family looked upon the fire as a challenge to rebuild a larger, better-equipped factory in which to produce their fine products—the crystal-encased lily-type flower designs that are captured in a variety of artistically formed ashtrays, ring holders, scent bottles, pitchers, vases, bookends, pen and candle holders, and lamps.

The backyard factory was an outgrowth of "Pop" St. Clair's after-hours artistic glass production while working for MacBeth-Evans. He loved to make weights to give to his friends. In fact, almost every fellow factory worker who ever did John B. St. Clair a favor received a weight in return.

The mastery of crystal-encased flower forms to make popular doorstops and paperweights came only with much practice and experimentation. The year 1938 saw the closing of MacBeth-Evans and a loss of jobs by Pop, John, Jr., Joe, Ed, and Bob St. Clair.

A small sheet metal building was erected in the backyard to house a one-ton capacity furnace and other necessary glass finishing equipment, and the St. Clairs were in production. The business boomed despite the fact that three of the boys had to leave to serve in World War II. With their return in 1945, an office display room was added (fortunately, in a separate concrete-block building which was not affected by the 1964 fire), and new products

Pop St. Clair, founder of the St. Clair Glass Works and father of the present owners.

The St. Clair brothers combine skills to make a miniature lily weight. Ed, on the right, inserts first air traps. Joe, on the left, blocks. Bob, at the rear, inspects a blocked weight before placing it in the electric annealing oven. (Photograph by George J. Melvin.)

were added to the output. All these products sell so rapidly from their showroom and through a very limited number of gift shops in the United States that no traveling sales representative is required.

The day-tank type of furnace in use before the fire held about one ton of glass. This is a sufficient batch, when melted, to produce 200 to 220 regular St. Clair paperweights a day for five days or 300 of the small (miniature) weights. Only two days' work of lamp parts could be made from a melt in this tank.

Because the annealing ovens are set to cool glass paperweights and lamp parts properly, the larger doorstops are no longer made at St. Clair. Joe said, however, that the loop design doorstops made by Pop St. Clair at MacBeth-

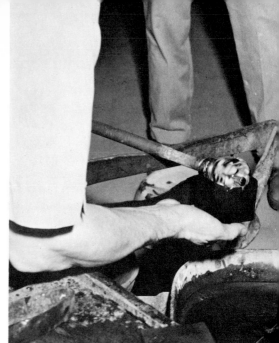

Edward St. Clair pierces air traps into the base of a molten glass paperweight. Joe St. Clair puts the finishing touches to blocking of a small-sized St. Clair crimp weight. (Photographs by George J. Melvin.)

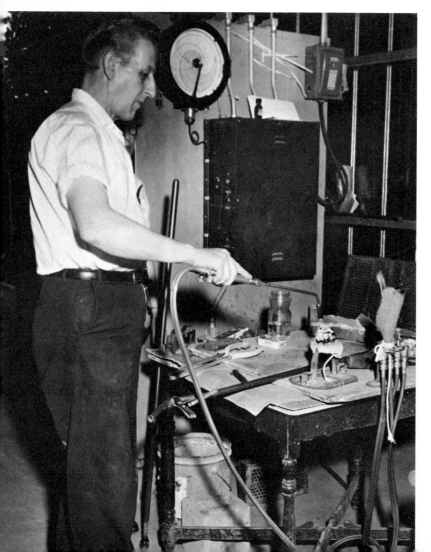

Bob St. Clair uses a torch to fire-polish the pontil break-off point at the base of a small-sized St. Clair weight. (Photograph by George J. Melvin.)

Evans about thirty years ago now bring a very high figure at antique shops. Joe recalled, "The largest doorstop my father made weighed eighteen pounds."

In June, 1964, during the Paperweight Collectors' Conference held at Neenah, Wisconsin, Joe presented to the John Nelson Bergstrom Art Center and Museum a doorstop made by his father, which weighed 11 pounds 14 ounces. It is made of crystal with blue-green base coloring and contains one large center bubble and six perimeter bubbles. He also gave the museum a weight, recently completed, in which a small pink-and-white ceramic pig stands in a field of green. This latter weight is to be seen in the display cases of the museum as No. 717.

A more recent product of the St. Clair Glass Works is an output of replicas of Greentown, Indiana. Produced are the holly amber toothpick holders; Greentown dog and the old woman's head (witch) match holders, pressed in the typical Greentown opaque green, caramel, and transparent amber glass; and several patterns of Greentown tumblers. Many fragments of Greentown glass were dug up from the site of the Indiana Tumbler and Goblet Company, Greentown, Indiana, which is not too far from Elwood. This cullet was ground and reworked in the above-mentioned molded pieces and also was used as a colorant within crystal lamp parts and paperweights. Pressed work is run only one month, then the factory returns to manufacturing weights.

Speaking of lamps, Joe remarked with a twinkle in his eye, "White is our best seller because the white lily design blends with any color scheme." He continued, "It's always interesting to watch prospective buyers view the lamps! The men select the more intense ruby, emerald, or cobalt, while the women are pleased with the pastel tints of yellow, spring green, powder blue, and delicate rose. When one partner will not give in to the other's opinion, the husband and wife end up buying the compromise, a white lamp."

These lamps, whatever the color, are a stimulating addition to the beauty of any color scheme. Joe pointed out, "Ruby, green, and blue flowers in the lamps outsell yellow, and for that reason few yellow lamps are made." Any collector who is the owner of a Greentown caramel fragment lamp or any of the St. Clair pressed ware made of Greentown green, amber, or caramel fragments, should be advised to cherish these, because securing of such cullet by digging is no longer permitted. Thus St. Clair 1964 reproduction Greentown holly amber and caramel rank among the very desirable reproductions to possess.

In looking about the St. Clair retail shop and display room, one is aware of the beauty, in both color and design, apparent in each piece displayed. The purchaser buys according to his individual likes as to color and the functional value of the wares purchased. All are equally well turned out, even on the production basis that results in large quantities of items being produced weekly.

Joe says with justifiable pride, "My dad worked out the very best system of weight making, and we follow it today." The system includes steps similar to those described in other chapters—yet each weight maker has his own individual tricks. The St. Clair factory's operating procedure is unique in that a five-man shop works each man at his own particular job to complete a given weight, where other weight makers individually do all steps required to complete any weight. The St. Clair Glass Works has a smoothly operating shop, and as Joe observed, "We need it, for we have considerable overhead in materials, fuel bills, and labor. Five families depend upon our factory for their livelihood."

Sometimes weights, such as their large red apples, have a series of very evenly spaced, minute bubbles showing close to the outer surface of the finished weight. These small air traps are put into the weight while it is still

Steps in making a St. Clair production weight. *Left to right:* (1) First gather plus colored bits, $1\frac{1}{2}$ inches diameter by $\frac{3}{4}$ inch high. (2) Second gather added over first plus three colored bit groups, $1\frac{1}{2}$ inches diameter by $1\frac{1}{2}$ inches high. (3) Third gather to case three bit groupings, $1\frac{1}{2}$ inches diameter by $1\frac{3}{8}$ inches high. (4) Air traps inserted—three in base, three in centers of bit color groups to form three lily flowers, 2 inches diameter by $1\frac{1}{2}$ inches high. (5) Final gather of glass to cover air traps before blocking, $2\frac{1}{2}$ inches diameter by $2\frac{1}{2}$ inches high. (6) Finished weight after blocking to make a regular spherical shape, $2\frac{1}{2}$ inches diameter by $2\frac{1}{4}$ inches high. (Photograph by George J. Melvin.)

St. Clair weights: bubble weights, crystal pears, and lilies. (Photograph by George J. Melvin.)

St. Clair paperweights: ceramic yellow-green frog encased in crystal, bell weight with five lilies, pear-shaped weight, pink sixteen-petal rose over deep green base. (Photograph by George J. Melvin.)

molten glass through the use of a ball-shaped bubble mold which contains a spike for each bubble made. Some refer to these weights as raindrop weights.

The attractive St. Clair bell-shaped weights require the use of a very small block to form the knob or top of the bell form.

In the case of the teapot ring holder, Joe applies a small crimped gather to form a handle, then a spout, and finally a top.

Joe patiently showed me a valuable shipment of gold used to make the ruby-colored flowers. When it is combined with opal white, it results in the

The St. Clair Glass Works of Elwood, Indiana, markets many beautiful production items including paperweights, miniature and regular size; bookends; pen holders; vases; scent bottles; ring holders; ashtrays; pitchers. (Photographs by Cloetingh and Deman Studios, loaned by Joseph L. St. Clair.)

delicate pink coloring so popular in St. Clair work. This gold costs forty dollars an ounce. Each ounce of gold foil must be carefully cut into minute squares ready for adding to a batch of glass which is melted in a small pot or crucible, not in the large day tank which holds a week's supply of crystal. "The gold–ruby-red is the most difficult of all glass colors to make," Joe declared.

Asked if St. Clair had ever produced roses, Joe said, "Yes, about one hundred of them to date, but the production of roses presented so many problems, we discontinued this weight for the present."

Speaking of glass batches and melting, Joe noted, "The recipe or formula for the mix is not so valuable as a knowledge of temperature control and timing."

Colors used by St. Clair are secured in part from the Kokomo Opalescent Glass Company. Sand comes from the famous Ottowa, Illinois, deposit, and soda ash is furnished from Detroit. The important thing about Kokomo colors is that they are coefficient with the St. Clair crystal. As any glass producer knows, this is a very big factor in producing durable ware.

At the St. Clairs' home in Elwood, Joe pointed out some of the glass production he has retained. Among the items was a rectangle of Corning's perfect crystal, $2\frac{1}{2}$ by 3 by $1\frac{1}{2}$ inches in size, given by Corning to John, Sr., while he worked at the MacBeth-Evans factory. A beautiful St. Clair table lamp containing pastel lily flower forms in pink, yellow, blue, white, and pale green dominates a living-room table. Weights, bookends, and ashtrays fit properly into the room's decor. Joe has many samples of the Greentown reproduction pressed ware which their firm made recently.

The St. Clair factory reopened for business on September 21, 1964. It is a spacious, sturdily constructed building, 40 by 96 feet, and completely fills the space from the old factory building to the street frontage of the plot. A most attractive turquoise sheet metal covering on the building makes this factory a modern shop of beauty.

The new day-tank-type furnace at St. Clair which holds a ton or more of glass is unique in design. Two openings into the tank permit easier access for two workmen. The glory hole at the end of the tank makes use of the most intense part of the gas flame.

While the work at the St. Clair factory progresses swiftly, it never seems hurried. Each man in the five-man shop does his portion of the weight making with dexterity and graceful execution. One young boy works at the rear of the new building breaking up larger chunks of colorants into the bit-sized pieces needed for weight production.

On the assembly line one man twirls the small first gather on the end of the pontil rod. He quickly picks up coarse bits by rolling the hot gather in a layout of white on the marver. After a warm-in period, the gather plus bits is marvered. Then multicolored bits are gathered and warmed in, and the total mass is shoved into a crimp. At this stage air traps are inserted in the foundation of the weight by a second craftsman working at a cradle. A second gather meanwhile is prepared by the first man, who shears off a small bit of molten glass in a metal dip mold or cup. This second gather is quickly picked up by worker number two, who adds additional air traps and design manipulations. Then Ed St. Clair takes the pontil to a second furnace opening, gathers the final or third glass gather, and carries the pontil to Joe's cradle, where Joe starts immediately to block the final weight form.

Upon completion of the blocking and cutdown, Bob St. Clair picks up the pontil, holds the rod in a vertical position, and inspects the weight as it cools enough to start the annealing process. Bob then carries the weight to an asbestos-wrapped ring where he taps the pontil, knocking off the finished weight so that it lands upside down on the asbestos ring. Here he applies fire polish to the pontil mark, using a torch flame; in some cases he stamps an identifying die with the initials STC on the base of the weight. Carefully this weight is transferred to the electric annealing oven. The empty pontil is returned to the first worker for a repeat of the entire process.

The electric annealing ovens are extremely efficient. Carefully controlled by thermostats, the temperature reduces from 900 degrees Fahrenheit until only a pilot heat remains in the oven. This permits such gradual reduction in heat and such expert annealing that the loss in production during this process of weight manufacture is reduced to almost nil at St. Clair.

Besides the small round die Bob uses for signing weights, which has only STC, there is a larger round die which reads "St. Clair." This is stamped on the finest of their production. Also used to identify St. Clair production is an oval paper sticker reading "Handmade, St. Clair, Elwood, Indiana." Not all pieces are identified when they are shipped. Some dealers prefer to have unmarked wares to sell.

Several St. Clair die designs enjoyed great popularity in the past. During the World War II years, the design containing a V with thirteen surrounding stars was a top seller—as was "Remember Pearl Harbor." Other St. Clair designs of this type include "My Little Niece" and "Merry Christmas and Happy New Year."

Decals have been successfully transferred to white opaque plates and enclosed in attractive St. Clair weights. These designs include A & W Root

Beer, Royal Jester, and a limited number of George Washington and John F. Kennedy weights.

Like the Degenharts, St. Clair at one time used small translucent crystal butterflies and bees coated with blue and black ground glass as design centers for fine weights. Joe explained that the colorful reds applied to these glass forms were unsuccessful as a rule because red burns out at 2100 degrees Fahrenheit.

Of St. Clair roses Joe said, "Roses are difficult to make. In fact, production problems limited our output. In my lifetime I hope to make five hundred, but only about one hundred have been completed." Among the St. Clair roses is the delicately beautiful, pink, sixteen-petal rose over a green base.

Another St. Clair weight, the frog, shows a wee ceramic frog sitting on a white base color surrounded by pale green, rose, blue, yellow, and white lily-form flowers encased in the clearest of crystal. Of the frog weights Joe remarked, "We made several, but I believe about four were successfully annealed. However, we shall try these again sometime."

Ed St. Clair has started production on a collectors' line of magnum-sized weights. These may contain the ceramic frog or dog, cat, mouse, lamb, or bear, to name a few. Then, too, Ed is using some cased colored-glass canes, which he secured from a retired glass craftsman of the Pittsburgh area, to make the star flower design which resembles the H. Miller patent design of 1890. Fortunately for serious collectors, most of Ed St. Clair's line of weights bear the identifying die, St. Clair, tapped into the pontil end of the weight while the glass is yet molten.

Recently a resident of Indiana reported to me that Robert St. Clair is making some paperweights with ceramic animals enclosed. He is signing them with a die which reads "Bob St. Clair."

Chapter 17

Joseph Zimmerman
and Gene Baxley
Corydon, Indiana

Victor Zimmerman, who was of French descent, started working in glass factories at Marion, Indiana, when just ten years of age and was engaged in glasswork all of his working years. Victor had experience in several factories, including Shreveport, Louisiana, and Alexandria, Indiana, at the Lippincott factory, before he joined the Corydon Enterprise. This was a lamp-chimney factory. In 1957 a stroke terminated all of his active glass production and caused a gradual decline in his health, resulting in his death March 20, 1964.

It was while Victor was working in the lamp-chimney factory at North Vernon, Indiana, that he and his wife Daisy were blessed with a son, Joe, born May 4, 1923.

In 1938 Joe Zimmerman started spending summer vacations as a glass-worker at Corydon Enterprise, putting crimps on the tops of lamp chimneys. He also helped his father with the weight making.

Joe started in earnest to master the skills of glass offhand production at the Glass Handicrafters, a Corydon factory where his father was chief glass artisan and Mr. James Yunker was the financial backer. Later, while his father lay ill, Joe worked constantly to improve his skill; then he took the pieces home for his dad's critical judgment and experienced advice about how to improve the glass products. Victor's advice was rendered not entirely from experience because he inherited from his father, Frederick Zimmerman, who had been an expert glass presser at the United States Glass Company

Joe Zimmerman, left, and Gene Baxley, right, at the door of their glassworks. (Photograph by the author.)

in Pittsburgh, Pennsylvania, an appreciation for good offhand glass and a schooling in the finer points of glass judgment.

Printed on a small tag, this description accompanied each handcrafted production as it left Glass Handicrafters of Corydon, Indiana.

A Modern Antique of Crystal Glass Handicrafters, Corydon, Indiana.

Modern antique manufacture began as an effort to re-introduce the solid glass paperweights made by English and Colonial Craftsmen for our great-great grandparents and now so eagerly sought after as collectors' items. Five years study and patient experimenting finally worked out all the involved processes by which Bristol, Sandwich and other early glass workers immured their lovely creations of colored flowers, laces and scrolls in solid crystals. This glass is truly "hand made." Each piece starting as a small nucleus of molten crystal is built up layer by layer of clear and colored glass, the colored glass particles being manipulated into position to form the design. The designs containing spheres, hollowed out and painstakingly coaxed into shape, become ash trays, vases and bottles. "Coaxed" is really the proper word, since after fifteen seconds the glass cools and must be reheated for several minutes before another step in the sometimes hours long process of making an individual piece is completed.

Modern antiques will always be in short supply since only a very small group of highly skilled gaffers know and can carry out the intricate manipulations involved in its manufacture. Every piece made is distinctive and most are exclusive creations made nowhere else in the world. With their ever intriguing designs ranging from delicate to bold, encased in thick gleaming crystal walls, modern antiques are conversation pieces today and will be prized antiques tomorrow.

Joe Zimmerman and his wife Callie are the parents of three children: Josie, Barton, and Kerry. Joe hopes one of these will be sufficiently interested in glasswork to make a fourth generation artisan.

Gene Baxley, like Joe, is a graduate of Corydon High School. He was born January 7, 1932, at Mount Healthy, Ohio, near Cincinnati, the son of Bertha Vausha Baxley and Earl Baxley. Gene trained in glasswork at Glass Handicrafters starting in 1958 under Joe Zimmerman's watchful eye.

As Joe explained, "You can't train a glassworker. He must love the work, the creative aspects of it, and above all be oblivious to the intense heat and difficult working conditions." An apt pupil and an enthusiastic worker Gene proved to be—to such a degree that these two young men joined in a partnership for the manufacture of a variety of types of offhand glass in the present Zimmerman Art Glass Company. On May 5, 1963, Joe Zimmerman and his partner Gene Baxley melted their first batch of glass.

Gene is widely read and philosophizes in his southern drawl, "The only limit to creative offhand glasswork is one's imagination. There is a new challenge to be met as each piece is made. We place every teardrop, or tiny bubble, in our ware with an individual prick of the ice pick. No molds are used. In fact, the only type of enclosure for a setup are these three harness rings which we use, filled with color, to make the lily designs found in doorstops, bookends, and weights. Otherwise all base color and design color is simply spread on the marver plate for pickup."

Gene has observed in the short history of this factory that spring is a good season to sell spring-green-colored weights, while fall is the time their luscious-looking apple and pear weights sell best. These two designs are different from fruit weights found in other factories in several respects. They are larger. They are finished with attractive green stem and leaf forms applied to the pontil end of the form. All veins in the leaves are individually pressed in with a putty knife.

Examples of Zimmerman production weights. *Left to right:* Blue-and-yellow crimped design called Pond Lily; morning glory blue-and-white flower; red apple with green applied stem and leaf; yellow pear with applied green stem and leaf; five pink petals centered to large bubble over light-green crimped base color, called Fountain. (Photograph by George J. Melvin.)

The tools in use at the Zimmerman factory are largely inherited or purchased from the Corydon Enterprise, together with the ice pick and putty knife mentioned before. However, in the hands of these inspired workmen, tools, hot glass, colors, and creative inspiration combine to produce some most interesting and individual products.

A look about the display-room portion of this factory reveals a variety of glass products including:

1. Lamps, finial, three center ball-shaped glass portions containing lily design, joined with brass findings and footed with an offhand four-loop glass base. All glass portions made offhand.
2. Crystal vases, birds, dishes, pitchers, "intoxicated gourd" (the glass oddity one buys for the person who has everything).
3. Weight construction used in production of
   a. Bookends—three-lily design in many colors.
   b. Doorstops—three-lily design or multiple-daisy design $6\frac{3}{4}$ to 7 pounds in weight.
   c. Pencil holders.
   d. Ring holders.
   e. Paperweight pitchers.
   f. Ashtrays.
   g. Three sizes of perfume bottles, decanter bottles, etc.
   h. A wide variety of paperweight designs weighing 4 pounds and up including:
      (1) Morning glory—a blue-centered, white-edged flower (resembling a large morning glory), one large center bubble.
      (2) Crocus—each petal of this white flower individually shaped, assembled as a crocus, and then encased in crystal.
      (3) Gardenia—white petals individually shapea, wide spread, in finished weight. Sometimes these flower weights are faceted.
      (4) Rose—Although he had been disappointed with past results from crimp roses, Joe has recently completed fine pink, yellow, lavender, and red rose weights.

(5) Aster—a cane setup with bubble center and small bubbles at the end of each cane (resembling exploding fireworks).

(6) Pond lily—five petals, one large center bubble (each depression in color made with a putty knife). Weights made in a variety of two-color combinations. While Zimmerman calls this a pond lily, the weight resembles more one made with a crimp to shape the base colors.

(7) Pentagon—a five-sided, double white cane, bubble air traps at each of five points over a white base.

(8) Red apple, yellow pear fruit weights—both with green leaf and stem.

(9) Ceramic animals placed over white or colored lily pad ground in blown encasement.

(10) Five-petal lily—large center bubble and smaller bubbles at end of each petal. This weight is called the Fountain by Gene Baxley.

(11) Butterfly—a small metal butterfly shape is coated with ground-glass particles, then encased over a multicolored or two-color pond-lily-type base.

Not all Zimmerman weights are identified; some few have a copper wire bent in the form of a written letter Z enclosed at the base under the base color. Others have a letter Z, which is tapped in with a die at the pontil end while the glass is still very plastic as a result of the fire polishing.

The first paperweight in which Joe Zimmerman placed any identification is a magnum weight with a multicolored base. Three small copper, glass-enameled butterflies hover over this base. This magnum weight is now in the collection of Dr. and Mrs. L. C. Thompson. The identification is a copper-wire Z placed at the base of the weight.

Zimmerman weights are made $2\frac{1}{4}$ inches, $2\frac{3}{4}$ inches, $3\frac{1}{2}$ inches, and $5\frac{1}{2}$ inches by size and from $\frac{1}{4}$ pound in weight up to $6\frac{3}{4}$ to 7 pounds for doorstops.

At the Zimmerman Art Glass Company the crystal batch is melted once each week in a day tank and allowed to settle one day while the boys

Zimmerman weights. *Left to right:* Ceramic squirrel in center on white crimped base; footed weight containing metal, glass-coated butterfly over blue and white base; pink eight-petal rose over green grass base; footed, white, eight-petal crocus-type flower over green grass base; double white cane pentagon loop design over opaque white base. (Photograph by George J. Melvin.)

go fishing. Then the work commences. Colors found in their output are rods purchased from the Kokomo Opalescent Glass Company, Kokomo, Indiana, and the Conlan Glass Company, Long Island, New York.

The general process of production weight making described by Joe Zimmerman by steps is as follows:

1. Small gather from furnace on end of pontil.
2. Pickup of finely ground base color, circular setup from marver or from a small tin can filled with color.
3. Warm in the color fragments.
4. Form design with putty knife.
5. Straighten up, cut down briefly with tweezers.
6. Second gather of glass from furnace.
7. Center bubble and any other desired air traps pierced with ice pick.
8. Third gather of glass.
9. Block.
10. Cut down, and warm in again.
11. Complete blocking and cutdown.
12. Crack off into sandpit.
13. Fire-glaze pontil mark or break off with intense torch flame.
14. Identify with Z die (very often this is omitted).
15. Place on asbestos carry-in paddle.
16. Place in metal box lined with rock wool.
17. Anneal in gas-fired oven.

Weights made at 6 A.M. daily anneal for twenty-four hours; those made at 2 P.M. anneal for sixteen hours. After the weights are removed and carefully examined, they are placed on the showroom shelves for sale. Joe says, "Seventy per cent of our sales are from our own factory to the tourist and to the collector."

When these young men become temporarily weary with their weight production, they branch out to crystal glass bell, chain, or cane work, or they make a Zimmerman twist crystal vase or a putty-knife ribbed, tall stemmed vase with paperweight-type base, which is Joe's favorite product. A weight design newly developed is a large blown bubble containing some miniature bone China flower or animal. The bubble seems to grow from a pond lily-type flower previously described and the entire design is then cased in crystal. These are collectors' weights in the magnum size.

As Gene Baxley said, "I haven't really worked one day since I came here. I love it." These are the young men to encourage. They are achieving highly artistic and desirable individually designed weights. The weights of these two men appealed particularly to the author because they are creatively inspired, dependent upon no molds, but rather upon the skill of the workers.

Designs created since I first researched this factory include a series of hand-painted designs created by Lucy Webb. These include many delicate butterflies and flowers. Frequently the butterflies are encased above a large yellow pond-lily-type flower base. Small ceramic yellow or pink roses are encased in the center bubble of white or green "pond lilies" to form one of Zimmerman's most popular designs. Other designs now crafted are called "Hearts and Lace," bell, and mushroom.

Part III

The Lampworkers

The

Lampworkers

Lampworking is a skilled craft requiring many years of training. Both lampworkers Ronald Hansen and Charles Kaziun will attest to this. The paperweights which these two gentlemen produce provide an interesting contrast in method of paperweight manufacture to those made by the pot workers previously described. Francis D. Whittemore prefers to be classified as an apparatus worker.

Lampworkers may be grouped in two divisions according to Charles Kaziun:

1. Lampworkers who use straight prefabricated glass rods or tubes to make glass products.
2. Lampworkers who combine glass-rod and molten-glass techniques to make glass products.

The reader may have been a fascinated onlooker at some exposition, fair, or educational exhibit where a lampworker was demonstrating his skill. This type of dexterous workman never fails to attract an interested audience wherever he may be. Heating prefabricated glass crystal or colored rods and manipulating the molten glass into intricate miniature novelties is a skill not too many men practice today.

Perhaps many more present-day lampworkers are exercising their skill in the manufacture of industrial and scientific apparatus. A fine description

Using the lampworker's hot flame and small tools, Harold Hacker produces miniature novelties

Lampworker John Bernardini of the Kimble Division of Owens Illinois at work in Vineland, New Jersey. (Photograph used through the courtesy of the *American Flint.*)

Harold Hacker at work at Knott's Berry Farm. Notice the spun glass ships, fish, and birds in the background. (Photograph by W. C. Nelson, Buena Park, California.)

of this type of lampwork is quoted with permission from the *American Flint* of March, 1960, as follows:

> Using a hot flame and small tools, the lamp worker fabricates with the skill of his hands and the breath of his lungs, intricate and technical scientific apparatus from glass tubing and glass parts.
>
> In the hands of scientists, researchers and students, the product of the lamp worker increases the knowledge and progress of man and brings improved health, a higher standard of living and increased security to all.

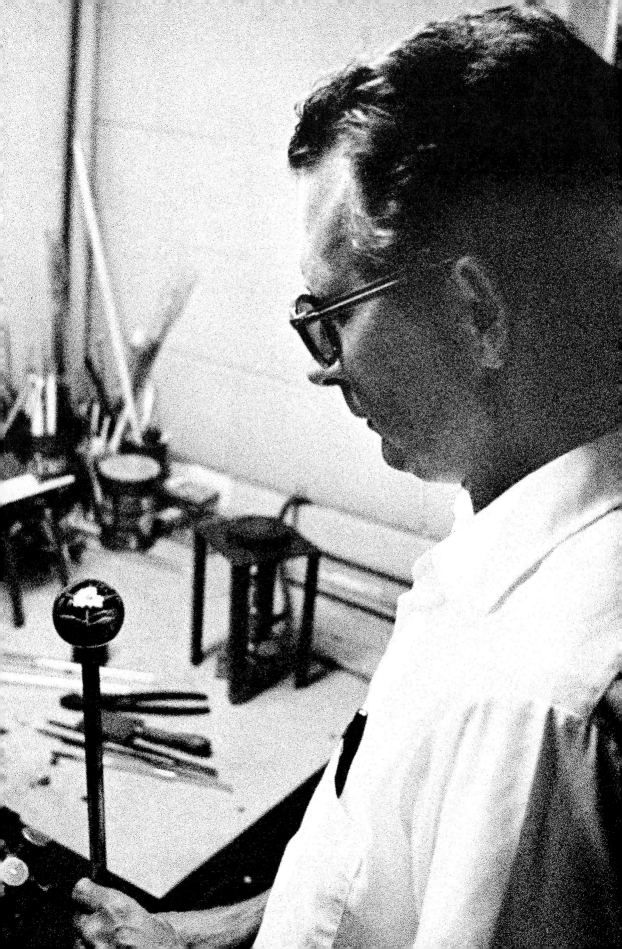

Chapter 18

Joseph S. Barker
Newark, Delaware

Through Ronald L. Gardner of Newark, Delaware, I learned of a newcomer to the lamp-glass paperweight trade.

Joseph Scalona Barker of Newark, Delaware, was born in Vineland, New Jersey, to Adelmina Scalona Barker and William Thomas Barker in 1933. He became interested in glass at age seventeen. His first employer in glass was H. S. Martin Company at Vineland, New Jersey. Next he was employed by Knotes Glass in Vineland. He alternated employment at these two factories, serving his apprenticeship and gaining all possible experience in glass.

In September of 1959 Joe Barker started work with a small glass firm in Wilmington, Delaware, and continued as an apparatus-glass craftsman until 1965 when he was promoted to plant manager.

A sampling of his weight designs include a dogwood complete with stem and leaves against a blue or green base color, five- and six-petal yellow or blue flowers on stem with leaves over blue base, and small red or black snakes placed over leafed branches against a white ground. He also makes a red poinsettia with green stem and a few leaves on an emerald green base color. The weights are miniature in size. Those I observed from Mr. Wiseburn's collection were signed on the color ground, "Joe Barker."

Mr. Gardner goes on to say, "Because of his interest and experience

Joe Barker inspects a finished weight in his home workshop. (Photograph by Ronald L. Gardner.)

in scientific glassblowing, Mr. Barker could not stay away from working with glass when his employment no longer required actual glassblowing. To satisfy his interest and because he likes a challenge, he decided to set up a working area in his basement and try his hand at paperweights.

"He attributes his decision to the suggestion of a brother-in-law who collects weights and convinced him that he should try it. The overriding reason, it appears, is that he was told that it would take many years to accomplish, and that it is obviously very difficult because there are only a few people currently making paperweights. This, I believe, is what made the decision. He had to try it.

"Studying examples of weights made by various artists and applying his knowledge and experience as an apparatus-glass craftsman Joe set about designing an efficient system to produce weights of high quality using both new and established methods.

"Recently he has been searching for the best available glass to achieve the colors desired and has been working on perfecting production techniques.

"Making one good weight or many does not satisfy him. He must know why they are good or which specific techniques result in good weights. Rather than continue and get the bad with the good, he stops his production efforts and spends his time on analysis of a 'failure' or a problem area. When the problem is solved production is resumed, but not before.

" 'This is a luxury you can afford when you are doing this as a hobby,' Joe says. 'I'd starve if this were my livelihood.' Frankly, it is not so much a hobby as it is a challenge. He enjoys the success of solving a problem as much as he does in making a good weight. In the area of analysis and design of systems and techniques, Joe gives much credit to Mr. Ralph G. Nester, his former employer, now retired, and a very close friend. He has been and continues to be, a real source of assistance and encouragement.

"Mr. Barker has marketed a few weights produced at home during his free hours away from his present employment as plant manager for a company which manufactures glass and electronic products.

"Joe and his wife Nancy have four children, three daughters and one son. The children are curious observers, but Nancy is an able assistant and is gaining a great deal of knowledge and interest in glass and paper-weight making."

Chapter 19

William F. Breeden
Elmer, New Jersey

William F. (Bill) Breeden, born September 5, 1900, at Millville, New Jersey, grew up with glass because his father was plant owner of the Eastern Glass Works, Millville, New Jersey. At thirteen years of age Bill left school to work in his father's plant and by age sixteen he had attained the rating of journeyman. He learned what he terms "lamproom trade" and soon was able to teach many others the fine art of creating hypodermic syringes. As he assumed greater responsibilities at the Eastern Glass Works he learned all the jobs of those employed there, that he might be able to do any glass job which he might expect others to accomplish.

With the invention and use of glass-pressing machines the bulk of the orders for the regular output at Eastern Glass was lost. To keep one hundred employees busy, Breeden turned, by 1923, to the manufacture of perfume bottles. During this period Bill designed the new bottles to be manufactured. In 1932 the Eastern Glass Works was closed.

As an avocation during his glass-plant years Bill Breeden had searched through South Jersey for examples of the early glass craftsmen's whimsy, pitcher, vase, or other offhand oddities output. This, then, in 1932 became his vocation. Only in the past ten years has Bill given glass manufacture, on his part, renewed thought. Finally he achieved a life-long desire—that of establishing a lamp-glass shop at his home. Each month's output shows

William Breeden with a weight just completed in his shop. (Photograph by George J. Melvin.)

improved skill. Designs of millefiori rods spaced in rings around a center rod or clusters of rods over yellow, blue, or rose backgrounds, which are then cased with crystal, constitute the present Breeden output. After an absence of forty-seven years from the lampworker's bench, Bill is glad to be back at his trade in creative endeavor.

Seven lamp weights made by Bill Breeden include colorful grounds on which millefiori rod segments are grouped. White friars rod designs are enclosed in the center weight. (Photograph by the author.)

Chapter 20

A. F. Carpenter
Pasadena, California

Like some other pot-glass workers native to West Virginia, A. F. Carpenter eventually migrated to California. Born in 1908 at Normantown, West Virginia, Mr. Carpenter started as a carry-in boy at the Weston Glass Company and later worked at the Louie Glass Company, both in Weston, West Virginia.

With his meager savings in his pocket, Mr. Carpenter went to New York City in 1937 where he answered an ad for lamp-glass workers. Under the helpful guidance of a German lamp-glass worker, Karl B. Mortz, he learned the lamp-glass skill enough to demonstrate at the New York World's Fair of 1939 and at the San Francisco Fair the following year. In later years, Mr. Carpenter practiced his skill in various laboratories including Stanford University under Doctor Lester M. Field and at California Institute of Technology under Doctor Roy Gould. He fabricated TV and other vacuum tubes needed for highly technical experiments. Much of his work was accomplished with the aid of a magnifying glass, which accounts for the intricate parts in his present-day paperweight designs.

A. F. Carpenter's paperweights, which for a period of three or more years were marketed by Harold J. Hacker, include designs in yellow and black spotted lizards, cobras, rattlesnakes, ribbon snakes, turtles, salamanders, red and blue poinsettia, and dogwood flowers. All are carefully crafted works of delicate design.

A. F. Carpenter, lamp-glass worker, crafts a weight. (Photograph by J. A. Hawkins Studio, Pasadena, California.)

Chapter 21

Harold Hacker
and Associates
Buena Park, California

When a schoolboy can earn more than his teacher, parents are hard pressed to keep a lad in school. Such was the case with Harold James Hacker, one of today's lamp-glass artists, whom one may have seen at work at Knott's Berry Farm in California. Mr. Hacker was born June 1, 1906, at Weston, West Virginia. Parents Brent and Flora Hacker had no argument to combat Harold's desire, at the end of six years' schooling, to "earn more than my schoolteacher."

At thirteen years of age, Harold Hacker entered the employ of Weston Glass Company, where he advanced from carry-in boy to pressing stems on champagne glasses from a gather from a pot of colored glass. It was at Weston that Mr. Hacker learned the art of gathering glass from the pot full of molten metal. Following a Weston plant fire, he was employed at West Virginia Specialty Glass as a gatherer and there he learned to blow glass.

While vacationing in California in August of 1936, Harold Hacker met a long-time friend and former glassworker from Weston, West Virginia. This friend invited Hacker to visit a nearby glass plant at Huntington Park where he was surprised to find that about half the workers were former friends from West Virginia. At about that time he took a position as

Harold Hacker, lamp worker, learned the pot method before developing skill in lamp glass. Working at his bench he creates minute setups to enclose in small paperweights. (Photograph by W. C. Nelson, Buena Park, California.)

gatherer and spare blower at Technical Glass Company in Los Angeles, California. While there, he decided to improve his chances for upgrading his employment by study in a government technical school at Downey, California. Work at Douglas aircraft machine shop was a result of this study. He gained experience on various machines at Fox Machine Shop— but Uncle Sam's call to duty came after eight weeks of employment. He served for two and a half years with the 14th Armored Division.

Back in California, Mr. Hacker decided to follow through with an early hobby—that of creating miniature glass objects by the lamp process. He had first practiced this hobby back in Weston, West Virginia, using an alcohol lamp and foot bellows. Both Mr. and Mrs. Hacker are lamp-glass artists but had to employ several other "home" lamp craftsmen to keep up the rapidly depleted stock on display at Knotts. During his twenty-one years of demonstrating lamp-glass work Mr. Hacker created the popular fish, boats, swans, horses, and elephants. Exhibiting such intricate glass examples as a coach and horses, a carrousel, or a minutely detailed sail-boat elicited so many tourist questions that Mr. Hacker removed most of these from display.

At one time Mr. Hacker received permission to erect and demonstrate from a tourist-attracting day tank and glass pot. Hiring two good, experienced workers, one pot and one day tank were constructed; both were filled and fired. Mr. Hacker laughs as he recalls what a terrible batch of glass they first concocted, full of seeds and cords. The workers, undaunted by their failure, swung from their pontils weirdly shaped vases which they

A snake, a turtle, and a salamander—all examples of Hacker's earlier craftsmanship. (Photograph by the author.)

Three Hacker weights include a yellow four-petal dogwoodlike flower with five green leaves and a stem over blue ground, a beautiful cluster of blue grapes over white ground, and a brilliant scarlet poinsettia with five green leaves and stem. (Photograph by the author.)

sold at $1.50 each—the nearby sign proclaiming "Genuine cord glass." After six months, the pot-glass work was discontinued.

Until his retirement on January 1, 1970, Mr. Hacker's work schedule was a very busy one. Each day, morning hours were devoted to perfecting and creating his miniature paperweights at a workshop near his home in Buena Park, California. Later hours were spent at Knotts.

Designs sold under his signature, but made by a craftsman associated with him, include flowers (the brilliant red poinsettia, made also in blue and yellow, and some four-petal dogwood), a few turtles, several hundred snakes, and a few salamanders. He has marketed some lizards, complete with tongue and minute feet and claws—so tiny that much of the crafting must be completed under a magnifying lens. These spotted lizards, made in a limited number, as are the cobra snakes, are the work of his associate craftsman. More recent designs include sulphides, crimped roses, encased ceramic figures, octopus weights, grape clusters, and weights with small cast copper shapes enclosed. Marlin fish, elephants, bird-on-a-nest, small insects, and the like, are also encased.

All these weights have been marketed under Mr. Hacker's signature. His work, and that of one of his associates, was reviewed in the 1968 *Paperweight Collectors Bulletin.*

Chapter 22

Ronald Hansen
Mackinaw City, Michigan

Ronald Hansen—a man who underestimates his own ability—has an excellent knowledge of other glassworkers and the history of glass to back up varied experience in glasswork.

Mr. Hansen was born in Virginia, Minnesota, June 23, 1910, where his father was a railroad station agent. When a lad of seven or eight, Ronald was walking along the railroad tracks and came upon two occupants of the then-famous hobo village (found in most rail centers) who were busily engaged in making glass ships from pop bottles which had been severed lengthwise. These men, who were using a charcoal fire and a bellows combined with their simple tools and creative skill to fashion the glass ships, were judged by Mr. Hansen to have been immigrants from Bohemia or Czechoslovakia. Hansen credits this experience as his first insight to creative glasswork.

During the twenty years Mr. Hansen lived in Virginia, Minnesota, and including two years in college, he could not definitely determine which creative artistic venture he would follow—glassblowing or writing poetry. Today he combines them.

Experience as director of the Neon Tube School at Detroit, Michigan, coupled with a vast experience as a glass-lamp worker who traveled as a demonstrator to fairs, expositions, and department stores, Mr. Hansen's understanding of the potentials of glass-lamp work is fabulous. He is thorough

Ronald Hansen of Mackinaw City, Michigan, holding one of his blue flower miniature weights. (Photograph by George J. Melvin.)

in his search for quality materials and, like other weight artisans, decries the lack of quality colorants and crystal. In fact, Mr. Hansen proposes to make his own crystal in the near future and toward that end has been stockpiling quality raw materials.

There is no question about the quality in Mr. Hansen's weights. They are unique. "No two are ever identical," says Hansen. "The margin of human error makes for differences in weights."

Working in his shop in Mackinaw City, Michigan, using a glass rod $1\frac{1}{2}$ inches in diameter and lamps, Mr. Hansen creates a wide variety of weight designs in many colors. There are brilliant flowers, ranging in color from deep cobalt to robin's egg blue, yellow, pink, or lavender. The flower, the snake, the animal, or perhaps a fluted spiral is in turn encased in brilliant crystal. Some designs in the lighter-colored flowers contrast sharply with the deep ruby and mauve-purple backgrounds, while other dark blue multipetal flowers contrast with pale blue and white backgrounds. Some of his weights are faceted and others are overlaid.

Small blue, rose, and pink roses are encased in small crystal balls mounted on an integral crystal foot. The larger flower weights are usually *not* footed. In fact, it is difficult to do justice to an accurate account of the variety of Mr. Hansen's designs because they are, as he says, ". . . each an individual creation. A weight is actually made in a short time, once the carefully constructed setup has been completed by hand."

The weights, when finished, are well annealed and resist chipping and cracking. Mr. Hansen demonstrated this by taking one of his beautiful weights and bouncing it on a concrete floor as if he were tossing a ten-cent rubber ball.

The majority of Hansen weights measure $2\frac{1}{2}$ inches in diameter or smaller. One larger weight which we saw was not a lamp weight, but was made from the crystal melt at the Zimmerman Glass Company at Corydon, Indiana, while Hansen visited Joe Zimmerman and Gene Baxley. These three men have a common aim in that all desire to build their weight designs and setups individually using no molds or crimps.

Ronald Hansen weights of fruit, flower, and snake designs. (Photograph by Taylor and Dull, New York, New York, used through the courtesy of Paul Jokelson.)

Asked if he knew what type of design he would create when he started to work on a weight, Hansen said, "Oh yes, you must have some preconceived idea of the weight you are about to construct." The fact that Mr. Hansen never ceases creative experimentation is apparent in the variety of existing designs. The lampworker uses a torch—as opposed to a glory hole or furnace—for heating a prefabricated rod of glass. His pontil is also of glass as opposed to the furnace worker's metal pontil rod. In the case of lampwork weights it is necessary to use an electric roller to support a pontil for any weight of $2\frac{1}{2}$ inches or larger.

As both lamp and pot glass weight artisans are quick to declare, the use of good materials requires a large investment of money. When added to this are the investment in skill and the cost of weights which are broken or destroyed because they do not please the weight maker (sometimes as high as twenty-eight out of thirty weights), then the collector may more readily appreciate why he pays the price he does for a Hansen weight. Ronald Hansen called it, "The canon of pecuniary waste."

Ronald Hansen has two brothers interested in glasswork. His brother Robert, of Bridgeport, Michigan, is said to be making paperweights with flower and reptile designs enclosed, but I have not yet seen any of them.

For a better understanding of Mr. Hansen and a finer appreciation of his work, read his article titled "Hidden Facets of a Paperweight" which appeared in the June, 1965, *Bulletin of the Paperweight Collectors' Association.*

Ronald Hansen weights of fruit, flower, and snake designs. (Photograph by Taylor and Dull, New York, New York, used through the courtesy of Paul Jokelson.)

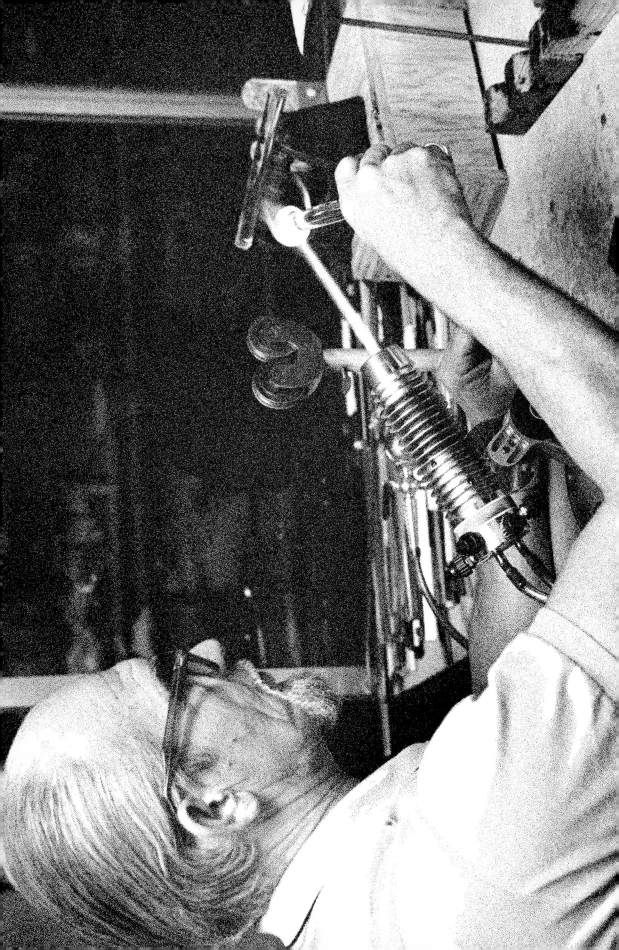

Chapter 23

William J. Iorio
Flemington, New Jersey

Iorio Glass Shop and Museum are located on routes 31 and 202 in Flemington, New Jersey. The museum houses two fine collections of cut glass and other glass items. Mr. Louis Iorio, dubbed "Mr. Cut Glass," was once an employee of the Empire Cut Glass Company, but with the closing of this factory in 1920, Mr. Iorio continued to ply his trade in a home shop. He taught his son, William J., and three grandsons his trade. Each one has developed the hobby of collecting different types of glass and cut glass, which items are displayed in William Iorio's museum.

He has collected for his museum representative examples of glass dating from 1500 B.C., a library of over 1,000 items, and 2,000 slides covering the subject of glass.

Only recently (since 1966), has William Iorio become interested in lamp work, technical production, and the making of lamp-type paper-weights. This experimentation would have been impossible without the help of two very cooperative lamp craftsmen, Jacques Israel of Pittsburgh, who made a wealth of information available to him, and a novelty-glass man, Ray Keller of Whitehouse, New Jersey.

Once informed about techniques, sources of supplies and tools, Mr. Iorio, with coaching from Keller, started to experiment with the difficult problems of coefficient of expansion and contraction, color intensities, and so forth. For about three years, he has made novelty spun ware and some

William J. Iorio works at his lampworker's bench in Flemington, New Jersey. (Photograph by Shepherd Studio, Flemington, New Jersey.)

White calla lilies with green stems and two large green leaves over cobalt blue background, signed "W. Iorio 1969." (Photograph by the author.)

blown ware using the lamp process. Paperweight buttons, earrings, and tie tacks are among his hobby productions made in millefiori, floral, gold inclusions, sulphides, and latticino designs since 1967.

In 1968, experimentation started on paperweights using flat floral millefiori setups on various background colors and carpets. A rose crimp

A five-petal flower ranging in color from blue to pink with a yellow center and green stem and leaves over a cranberry base color signed with chemical stamp. This weight has a domed top with sides ground into cylindrical shape. (Photograph by the author.)

used repeatedly produced on the thirty-first trial a delightful miniature fifteen-petal pink footed rose paperweight—a proud possession of the author. Designs which Mr. Iorio feels he has successfully made include flat florals in dogwood, clematis, daisy, and pansy plus small fruit and snake weights and millefiori setup designs.

William Iorio was born in Flemington, New Jersey, on January 21, 1914. He always has been interested in glass and is a skilled cutter and engraver. Now he is also a partially self-taught lampworker.

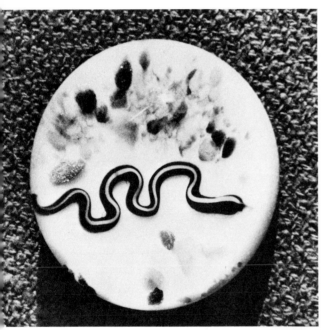

Brilliant color and gold stone bits over a white ground serve as a carpet for a white striped black snake, with acid etched Iorio signature. (Photograph by the author.)

A ten-segment millefiori rod segment random arrangement over black base color accented with gold stone bits signed "W. Iorio 1969." (Photograph by the author.)

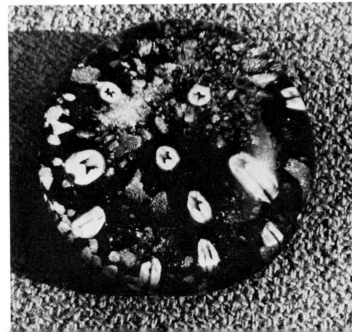

Chapter 24

Charles Kaziun

Brockton, Massachusetts

Charles Kaziun was born to Charles and Mary Kaziun at Brockton, Massachusetts, on May 18, 1919. His father was a shoemaker working in a Brockton factory. Both parents were immigrants from Lithuania.

One of the big events in the lives of Brockton inhabitants was the annual Brockton Fair. While a grade-school pupil Charles Kaziun attended this fair and saw a most fascinating exhibition of glassblowing. When in 1933 this type of fair exhibit returned to the town, Charles was a freshman in Brockton High School.

As Charles Kaziun tells it, "My parents could not understand my daily request for one dollar (a sizable sum in depression days), which was the admission price to the fair. Nor could they guess how I spent my time at the fair from its opening to its closing hour each of the six days. The truth was I was watching every movement and operation of the members of the famous Howell family as they demonstrated so skillfully their trade of ornamental lamp-glass creations." This display of skill motivated Kaziun to experiment at home. Experiment he did—using many colors of discarded household bottles and a couple of coffee cans converted into crude benzene burners. "With very little knowledge of glass chemistry, some of these unusual glass experiments succeeded rather well. I wouldn't attempt such combinations today," says Kaziun.

Each year at Brockton Fair time Charles Kaziun returned to watch the Howell family perform their miracles with glass and lamps. In time

Charles Kaziun at work in his shop. (Photograph by Harold E. Davis.)

Kaziun's gaze was so noticeably intent as to become annoying to the Howells, and they finally would do no demonstrating in his presence. This situation brought about a clever scheme upon the part of Charles Kaziun—he secured employment in a booth just opposite the Howell's so he could better watch their skill. They had no choice then but to perform for the admission guests.

With the completion of high school and graduation in 1937, the self-taught glassblower, Kaziun, secured employment in New York City. An important outgrowth of this employment was the development of speed in working with glass. Following this brief sojourn in New York, Charles Kaziun returned home to Brockton where he continued to do lampwork for a few customers.

Another avenue of lampwork was opened to Kaziun when an antique dealer brought him a glass button and asked to have it copied. This might have proved to be a popular business if the antique dealer had secured a sufficiently large number of buttons to market as frequently as he chose to do so. But Mr. Kaziun's integrity in marketing only perfect work limited the output. The fact that the dealer gave Kaziun neither credit for the production nor a fair price for any of the buttons brought this association to a speedy termination. This experience proved ultimately to be Kaziun's gain. His beautiful, jewel-like buttons, made for collectors, as well as earrings, lapel pins, and tie tacks highlight many of today's costumes.

After a discouraging period of economic want, Charles Kaziun heard that the Howell family, whom he had watched so closely at the Brockton fairs, was seeking a lamp-glass worker. This job, which Kaziun got, offered both security and an opportunity to gain training. "The Howells were the very finest type of people," says Kaziun. "They were strict—unbelievably straitlaced. They did excellent ornamental glasswork individually and as a family and expected the same from me. In addition to the regular exhibition work, I was permitted to do much creative experimentation in free time." Charles's objects created in off-hours were offered for sale at the next show only if perfect enough to pass the critical eye of Mr. Howell. Mr. Kaziun credits much of his present skill to the strict disciplining of the Howells during his association with this widely traveled family. As Kaziun says,

The unique and rare rose design with four green leaves, triple-cased or overlaid, and then faceted is one of Charles Kaziun's finest weights. (Photograph by Gordon N. Converse, Chief Photographer, *The Christian Science Monitor.*) Charles Kaziun snake weight. Yellow snake with red stripes on broken lace over amethyst ground. The snake has black head with green eyes. (Photograph from the collection of the John Nelson Bergstrom Art Center, Neenah, Wisconsin.)

"It is very hard for the beginner in lampwork to throw away his creations—but the Howells never sacrificed perfection." Mr. Kaziun speaks with sincere admiration for the fine work done by this family in their several endeavors: one daughter performed for some time as a demonstrator for school audiences, and the family was popularly received at the 1939 New York World's Fair. "Mrs. Howell at eighty-five years of age is still a superb lamp-glass worker," says Kaziun.

One of Mr. Kaziun's glass buttons and a glass figurine which he called Goddess of the Hunt came to the attention of Mr. James D. Graham, the noted biologist and skilled lamp-glass worker of the University of Pennsylvania. Upon meeting the creator of these fine examples of lamp-glass work, Mr. Graham was amazed to find that Mr. Kaziun was working without benefit of any nearby glass factory or glass artisans. Such self-attained perfection of products led Mr. Graham to employ Mr. Kaziun in 1942 as a lamp-glass worker for the University of Pennsylvania. This association was a most fortunate one for Mr. Kaziun. Mr. Graham was a fine teacher. He encouraged

Charles Kaziun to experiment and to market his products, but more important Graham gave freely of his advice and frequently his moral support.

As Kaziun experimented and took his products to Mr. Graham for critical appraisal, he heard first, "Yes, it is good, but the French—" As he experimented further for perfection in work, Mr. Graham next commented, "It is good, but the French signed their work." This humorous way of goading, plus constant encouraging to keep Kaziun trying to achieve the finest work, is credited today by Kaziun to be the basis for his ability to cope with each production hurdle.

The problem of working out a signature cane was a difficult one to solve. Usually only the most experienced glassworker has a knowledge of how far to extend a gather of glass to make a good glass cane. As many as eleven men working together, in step, have been said to pull a millefiori cane a distance of fifty to one hundred feet. Lacking eleven helpers and the know-how, much experimentation went into Mr. Kaziun's K signature cane which in time he learned to extend six feet, the distance of his arms' reach. As Mr. Kaziun puts it, "I believe that I am the only lampworker that has ever made canes in this country and possibly the only one to make the sharp crisp millefiori in all types: geometric, figure, etc."

During the five years Mr. Kaziun spent at the University of Pennsylvania, he was a regular weekend visitor to Emil Larson's home in Vineland,

Two footed weights from the collection of Mrs. Charles Kaziun. (Photographs by the author.)

Two snake weights from the collection of Mrs. Charles Kaziun. (Photographs by the author.)

New Jersey. They had much in common. Larson was fascinated with his conversations with Kaziun. Kaziun says, "Larson was very nice to talk with—a real gentleman."

It was at Larson's home that Charles Kaziun saw his first Millville rose paperweight. He was absolutely fascinated by this product and could scarcely wait to get back to his laboratory to try one. He had no idea how to make a rose but speculated on how it should be done. When he showed his attempts to Mr. Graham, the judgment voiced was, "You've tackled a tough one." While Kaziun visited Mr. Larson very often, no hint of how to make a rose was ever offered, and Kaziun knew better than to ask so skilled a weight maker his secret. Kaziun says, "It took me what would total three years of experimentation time together with three thousand dollars to perfect a Millville-type rose for a paperweight that could be made alone." Emil Larson did help Kaziun in many ways. Of Mr. Larson Kaziun says, "He is one of the few living glassblowers who could do match work. He worked in many of the eastern coast glass factories matching glass pieces. Prior to his retirement, he was one of our most skilled American gaffers."

Charles Kaziun double overlay weight in yellow containing pink rose with four green leaves, star-cut base, signed K where leaves join on base. Double overlay weight in dark gold-ruby, containing spaced millefiori setups in green, red, and white on light-blue opaque ground. Signed with K in setup on base of weight. (Photographs from the collection of the John Nelson Bergstrom Art Center, Neenah, Wisconsin.)

It was Emil Larson who gave Charles Kaziun faith that if he were good, he could make a living in creative lamp-glass work.

During these frequent visits to Vineland, Kaziun met another man who proved to be of tremendous help to him. The man was August Hofbauer. Hofbauer became so interested in the fine quality of Kaziun's work that he did all in his power to help Kaziun succeed, even to building a glass furnace in Brockton for Kaziun. Hofbauer shared secret glass formulas that had been in his family for 150 years for various purposes such as blowing, pressing, tube work, and color mixing. This was all the more unusual because as Kaziun put it, "The old-time German glassblowers did not usually take to others."

Hofbauer gave Kaziun much more than formulas. From his great knowledge of glass he related, besides recipes for various batches, exact temperatures and production controls—in fact, he explained in detail how each glass type and color had to be handled. Kaziun recalls how Gus Hofbauer controlled temperature without benefit of a pyrometer. The melting pot with its batch of glass was judged hot enough when Hofbauer could no longer distinguish the outline of the pot. Often he would thrust his bare arm into an annealing oven and withdraw it quickly. If his arm "bit" from the heat, the temperature was judged hot enough.

Temperature control is most important in all good glass production. Kaziun explains that too hot a temperature can burn out the red of the costly gold-ruby glass and some other colors as well.

The right colors must be stockpiled. Some of the best colors are the result of a mistake in mixing. Kaziun has studied the chemistry of glass and of all its colors. He at times compounds some of his colors. When he orders colors for his use from others, he directs exactly the ingredients and methods of mixing the needed colorants. These colors form a tremendous range for which price is of no consequence. Kaziun's aim is always to approach and sometimes surpass the excellent colors of the French weights. Some of his finest glass color was imported from France in 1880—a supply he hates to think of attempting to duplicate, once it is gone. "Colors in paperweights must be quite rich, and I believe the door is shutting on available sources for these rich colors," says Kaziun.

A Charles Kaziun crocus. The delicately shaded petals on this and the Kaziun tulip make these designs much sought after by discriminating collectors of contemporary weights. (Photograph by Harold E. Davis, courtesy of Charles Kaziun.)

"One can only speculate on how our predecessors learned that different colors could be made with the additions of metals. How did they discover that burned bones made white or sawdust made amber?" questions Kaziun.

Mr. Kaziun states, and I believe other weight makers would be quick to agree, that pride in workmanship and pride in quality products have fallen so short of the high standards existing prior to World War I that it is difficult today to get good materials and colored glass to use in the manufacture of quality glass objects. Kaziun also indicates that ability to secure color materials of excellent quality has steadily decreased, to a small extent after World War I and to a much greater degree since World War II.

One has only to view a button, weight, or scent bottle created by Charles Kaziun to realize that he demands the best in raw materials. He, in turn, unites these materials with an ability unequaled in our time into objects breathtaking in sparkling brilliance and grace.

"A good crystal," Kaziun says, "is difficult to make." It requires quality raw materials: the best sand, obtained from either the Ottawa, Illinois, or the Mapleton or Berkeley, West Virginia, deposits; the best in chemicals; and all other raw materials carefully compounded and melted in a good pot. Any hint of iron in a pot will discolor the mixture. The molten glass should be as free from seeds as possible. These fine bubbles are a cause of much concern in crystal batches. Bubbles in a weight which are purposely placed as dewdrops on the design enhance the value of a paperweight—but the seeds and blisters which occur in some weights apart from the design are definitely objectionable.

Another common pitfall in working crystal glass over color designs in paperweights is the appearance of fine cords or wavy lines called striae. They are frequently spiral, threadlike striations, produced sometimes by the manner in which a weight is worked, sometimes by the nature of the crystal in the pot. "The objection to cords in glass is the interference they cause with the optical qualities of glass," Kaziun comments.

None of these flaws is found in Kaziun's work, turned out at his studio shop in Brockton, Massachusetts. Not all of his production is perfect, but Charles Kaziun is a perfectionist. He markets only those products which he considers to be the best he can make. Many a collector has placed the work

Two examples of Charles Kaziun paperweights. Note the turtle, the shamrock, and the heart designs incorporated in his personally constructed millefiori canes. The white twisted background setup is referred to by the craftsmen as muslin. (Photographs by the author.)

of Charles Kaziun on a par with, or superior to, the workmanship and brilliance of the fine French weights of the past.

It is difficult for the average viewer of Kaziun weights to believe that a sizable portion of his production is discarded as imperfect. Kaziun says, "If ninety per cent of my glass production were correct in every detail, I would be happy." Glass must be worked at a reasonable heat, and the color must be right. Kaziun says he is his own severest critic. If final effect is not as he desires, he does not show the work. "The closer one comes to perfection, the more difficult perfection becomes," says Kaziun. "The last ten per cent is the moment of truth."

Another factor contributing to Kaziun perfection is knowledge of glass furnaces and their uses. Glass furnace types vary with their uses. The usual heating furnaces include these types: (1) the pot, (2) the day tank, (3) the continuous tank. The pot may be an open type like a crucible, or the furnace may have in it a container called a pot that can be closed to keep fumes from the fuel from affecting the glass. The shape may be round like a conventional crucible, or it may be oval like a bathtub. The day tank is

Charles Kaziun perfume bottle with blue lily and four narrow green leaves on gold-flecked pink base. Same design in stopper, which is a subminiature weight in itself. Gold K signature in center of bottom of base of both bottle and stopper. Both faceted. Perfume bottle with full blown pink rose and four leaves in base of bottle. Same rose also in stopper. Each with K signature where leaves are joined. Perfume bottle of clear crystal with white rose and four green leaves in base of bottle. Steeple stopper containing white flower with elongated petals and four green leaves. Signed with K setup on base of bottle and stopper. (Photographs from the John Nelson Bergstrom Art Center, Neenah, Wisconsin.)

a furnace in which the furnace is also the glass container. The name derives from the fact that the usual practice is to fill in and work out the glass each day, filling in at the end of the day and melting overnight. The continuous tank is a furnace in which the raw material is fed in at exactly the same rate as the melted glass is worked out. As the name implies, it is run continuously until worn out, for restarts are very costly. Batch material is usually fed in one end, and the glass is extracted from the opposite end. A glory hole is a smaller furnace with a much more intense heat used for reheating glass so that it may be worked by hand more easily. The annealing furnace is an oven into which all glass paperweights must be placed for a very gradual cooling.

Building a glass furnace can be very costly, especially if it does not function for a very long period of time. Some glass pots have been known to crack when first heated, while others may last up to five or six months. Kaziun quoted Emil Larson as estimating that one of the glass furnaces at the Pairpoint factory cost one dollar for every brick. In Mr. Kaziun's experience, a pot in the furnace in his shop may last a day, a week, two months, or perhaps longer.

As one understands the background of Charles Kaziun's self-schooling in chemistry, his experimentation in crafting glass, his search for quality raw materials, and his knowledge of furnaces and annealing processes, one can appreciate the full story behind the perfection of his weights. Only one process is added to his finished weights—that is grinding. In some cases, as in double and triple overlay, the paperweights are faceted. Prior to the present time, this work was done by others for Charles Kaziun. With the death of Carl Banks, a Pairpoint-trained grinder, and the death of his young, carefully trained protégé Henry Roderick, the number of skilled cutters in New Bedford was reduced to one, Tom Connelly. For this reason, Charles Kaziun has installed cutting wheels and proposes to learn the fine art of cutting and faceting weights, in order to complete his own work should all the trained glass cutters disappear from the scene. He explains his shop thus, "I am now set up to cut and grind in my shop. This gives me a completely integrated setup and is unique, I think, for a one-man shop. I can melt, work, and where necessary, finish by cutting all under one roof."

For what should one look in Kaziun production?

There are buttons and earrings—glass buttons of all descriptions and colors, some overlaid—all beautiful, $\frac{1}{8}$ inch to 1 inch in size. Designs include roses, lilies, millefiori, gold foil, and silhouettes.

Paperweights are made in many sizes. The subminiature size is the smallest, starting at about 1 inch in diameter. The largest weights approach 3 inches in diameter. Some are footed, some are on a pedestal, and some have a flat base. Designs enclosed may include millefiori, muslin with millefiori, individual snake, or flower. Most recent Kaziun weight designs enclose fruits and vegetables. Kaziun says, "I believe that I was the first and probably only one to make all of the various type of weights after the French school like millefiori; crown; flower; silhouette; overlaid or more accurately cased, footed, and plain; fruit and vegetable; reptile; and fish; both where setup is flat and in three dimensions. The animal canes are unique with me in this country."

Some of the flower weight designs include the wild rose, rose, daffodil, pond lily, narcissus, hibiscus, tulip, pansy, dogwood, and others. Animal and bird designs include twenty-four different animals; the duck, turtle, rabbit, heart, or clover enclosed in a cane are frequently centered in a weight. Other silhouette designs include Sun Bonnet Sue and Princess Eugenia. Many of the above-mentioned designs are made even more beautiful with the addition of a latticinio base or a base coloring which includes gold-stone flecks. The weights gain additional value and charm with each color overlay or casing which may be applied, coupled with the faceting of a top and five- or six-side punties or windows. Some even have a cut-star bottom.

Scent bottles varying in height from approximately 2 to 8 inches contain designs similar to those in some previously described weights. The scent bottles which are made with spherical stoppers have a matching design in the bottom of the bottle. A particularly graceful scent bottle is the tall one called Steeple Top, which contains beautifully constructed pink or white roses in both portions of the bottle.

No color work has proved to be too difficult for Charles Kaziun, the very earnest student of glass chemistry. Perhaps the most popular color is his gold ruby, found in the Millville-type rose, but one should look too at the beautiful yellow, pink, and white roses; the yellow daffodil on a cerulean-blue background, the white narcissus on an unusual amethyst base color, the rose-colored hibiscus, and the variety of tulip colors. Other colors used in designs include the yellow snake with black stripes and head and the red snake with black stripes resting on a green jaspered ground. Millefiori setups are charming with their many rainbow-hued canes, all made by Kaziun. Kaziun states, "I was the first in recent times, since the thirties,

Examples of Charles Kaziun's button designs.
(Photographs by the author.)

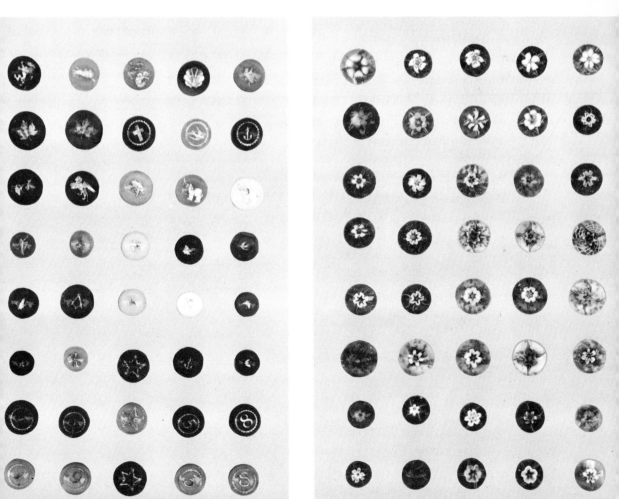

to make fine weights of collector quality and in all the classic types, as well as a few original innovations such as the triple-cased and the tilted and footed, and perfumes and colognes with *all* the types of setups. Another innovation includes flowers like the jonquil, which design incorporates both the flat type of setup as well as the third dimensional type in the flower trumpet part, and also flowers made in the peachblow and Burmese colorings."

All of the above productions cannot be adequately described by word pictures, and none but the finest color photographs can show the true colors used.

How does Charles Kaziun make a weight? Kaziun works in the privacy of his workshop at hours unlikely to be interrupted. One cannot wonder that the secrets acquired after such extensive practice, research, and experimentation are jealously guarded by the craftsman. Suffice it to say that Kaziun products are made of carefully planned and executed setups laid on crystal or colored grounds and finally encased in layers of the purest, brilliant crystal. In some cases these products are cased with additional layers of colored glass. Casing or overlaying is very difficult to complete successfully. Kaziun says that chances of perfect completion of a single overlay weight are 50–50; a double overlay is successful 1 out of 4 tries; a triple overlay 1 out of 9 times tried.

Kaziun, best known as a glassblower and a lampworker, is also a skilled pot worker. He uses the intense heat of many gas burners concentrated to one point for a portion of his lampwork while another portion of

Pink convolvulus with yellow edging and green leaves on fan trellis over aqua on alabaster ground. There is a 24K gold moth on the flower. (Photograph by the author.)

Lavender crocus with striated leaves on muslin ground with gold bug. (Photograph by the author.)

the glass is melted in a furnace. Together with all other components previously mentioned, the careful use of lamp, furnace, and annealing oven must be added to the list of skills necessary to complete Kaziun production successfully.

His particularly minute, perfectly formed signature K cane is inserted in every marketed product, usually in the base. However, each type of weight made by Charles Kaziun has a distinct signature. For instance, flower weights have the K cane placed in the bottom of the design. The K is surrounded with 5 to 10 miniature red hearts. In the case of the rose this signature forms a center for the flower's four green leaves. Millefiori weights have a K signature cane in the center of the setup. Scent bottles contain the gold K signature cane in both the stopper and the bottom of the bottle. Great variety is attained by Kaziun in identification of his work as well as in weight designing. It would be helpful if all weight makers identified their work as meticulously as Kaziun does.

There is no exclusive dealership for Kaziun weights. As to the sale of his weights, Kaziun says, "At first, I wasn't approached for an exclusive dealership, and now with all my collector patron friends it would not be fair to those that encouraged me when I first began and needed their good wishes."

Charles Kaziun and his pleasant wife, Louise MacBeth Kaziun, have two young children—a daughter, Mary, and a son, Charles. The only

A contemporary millefiori weight by Charles Kaziun. (Photograph by the author.)

weight Kaziun has named to date is a beautiful one called "Mary" for his daughter, which he made on the day she was born. It is a pink fourteen-petal rose with four green leaves, surrounded by eight white canes all resting on a light-blue ground and encased in purest crystal.

More recent Kaziun designs include a three-dimensional wild crocus in five colors (as pink, white, lavender, yellow, and turquoise) in a two-inch weight. A new rose design may include three, four, or five Sandwich-type roses over a muslin base in a two-inch weight. He is also making a colorful pansy and a popular convolvulus on a trellis.

Reminiscent of the French weights made at Clichy and Baccarat, Kaziun is combining in paperweights ten pictorial millefiori canes, the centers of which may contain fish, rose, clover, blue or red goose, duck, heart, shamrock, turtle, horse head, or rabbit. Even though the rods have been previously crafted by Kaziun, the setup of the small segments and completion of this type of weight require much time and dexterity on his part.

The later snakes by Kaziun may be either red or yellow, crafted in the manner of the French lizard weights. The snake gazes at a butterfly which hovers over a crocus.

No perfume bottles or buttons have been crafted by Charles Kaziun since 1964, but with the completion of a new shop realignment, he will once again create these products.

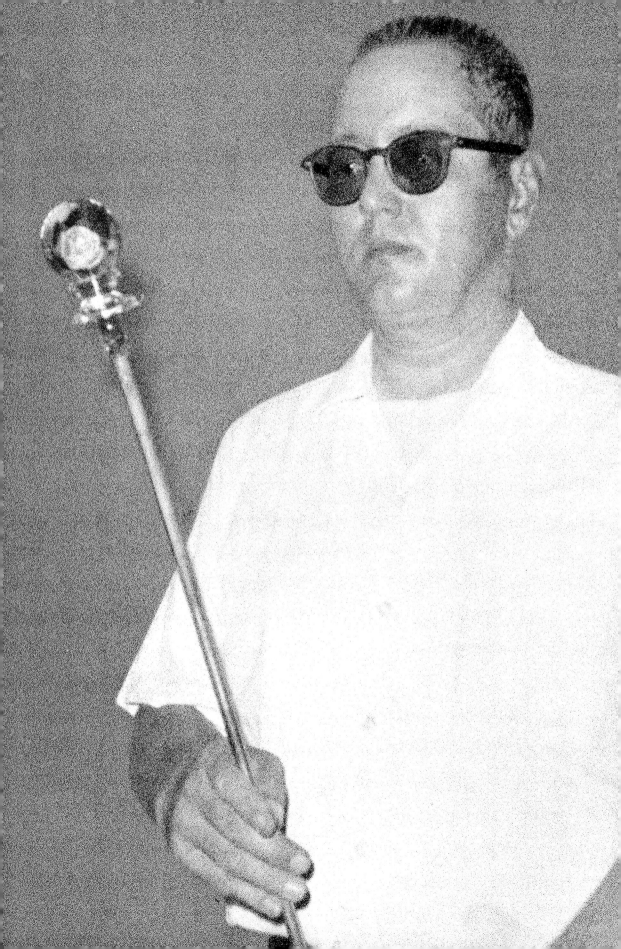

Chapter 25

Francis Dyer Whittemore, Jr.
Lansdale, Pennsylvania

A question from a student in Mr. Francis Whittemore's class kindled his interest in paperweights and his search into the methods of constructing them. Employed as a teacher in Salem County Vocational Technical Institute, Salem County, New Jersey, Mr. Whittemore instructed young men in the technique of scientific glassblowing that they might be better prepared to take places in today's industries. When questioned about weight making early in 1964, Mr. Whittemore drew upon his years of experience as a scientific and ornamental glassblower to develop tools and techniques of fabrication.

Thorough study of examples both old and modern led Whittemore to try making the smaller types of weights similar to those made by other contemporary apparatus-glass craftsmen. Says Mr. Whittemore, "After experimenting with a number of techniques for approximately three months, I developed a procedure which has been satisfactory in crafting weights. Now I am working to perfect glass colors and to solve a few production problems which need further refining." Recent research has been expended upon methods of making sulphides and other inclusions for weights, as well as casing and cutting techniques.

Could all paperweight collectors see the very early attempts of Mr. Whittemore as compared with the products marketed currently, they would certainly agree that he has made vast progress in crafting weights in a rela-

Francis D. Whittemore completes a footed rose weight. (Photograph courtesy of Francis D. Whittemore.)

tively brief time. Of course, such progress would have been impossible had Mr. Whittemore not been an expert glassblower when his interest in paperweights was aroused.

Francis Dyer Whittemore, Jr., was born in Hackensack, New Jersey, January 6, 1921, the son of teacher-chemist F. D. Whittemore, Sr. The family moved almost immediately to New England.

At seventeen years of age Francis Whittemore became interested in glassblowing as a hobby, but he soon embraced this skill as a vocation. Two years following graduation from high school he spent in study at Harvard University before he entered military service. Twenty-seven years' experience as an apparatus-glass blower has been a great assistance in making paperweights. For years Whittemore has made ornamental glass models to the scale of 1 inch equals 1 foot, complete in every detail. These miniatures include animals, goblets, pitchers, and decanters, to mention only a few. These

Francis D. Whittemore's footed, fifteen-petal, pale-pink rose weight with three green leaves at base. These are more often made with four green leaves at base. Another crimp used earlier by Mr. Whittemore has a center resembling unopened petals. Signed with W cane at base of leaves. (Photograph by George J. Melvin.) A tilted pink rose with four green leaves on crystal pedestal. (Photograph by the author.)

Francis D. Whittemore holds a tilted pink rose pedestal weight. (Photograph by the author.)

were judged by viewers to be examples of expert craftsmanship. Whittemore makes his own glass tools and crimps. He experiments with glass melts and is a very proficient, self-taught student of glass chemistry.

Currently his weights, made in sizes which vary from the subminiature measuring 1 inch in diameter to the largest which measures 3 inches in diameter, contain rose designs in blue, pink, white, yellow, or ruby with four green leaves. Some of his earliest roses were made with three leaves. In each weight a W cane signature appears at the conjunction of the leaves at the base of the rose within the sphere.

Prefabricated crystal is used by Mr. Whittemore to make casings for his flowers. His weights are in brisk demand by collectors who wish to add examples of the craftsmanship of this weight maker to their collections.

Francis D. Whittemore gave up his commercial employment in 1968 in favor of self-employment. This permits him ample time to experiment and to craft many new paperweight designs. He is now creating ten-petal blue flowers, ageratum, cornflower, and delicate sprays of flowers encased in pure colorless crystal. Other flower designs include pansy, rose (in many colors), rose with bud, jonquils, lily of the valley, calla lilies, daisies, tulips, crocus, and the poinsettia. Many weights are crafted without a base or carpet color. Some of these weights are on a pedestal; some designs are footed.

The same fine crystal used to encase his lamp setups is also being used by Whittemore to craft interesting pear and grape shapes, elephants, mice, whales, cats, owls, turtles, and snails. These whimsies measure about three inches in height and weigh about a half pound each.

Mr. Whittemore was fortunate to find an expert glasscutter who enjoys faceting his weights in an unusual manner. The unusual carrousel and star cuts enhance the beauty of Whittemore paperweight designs.

Francis Whittemore is trying his hand at encasing sulphide designs, some in white and some in color portrait heads. Musical instrument designs have also been enclosed. He has gained the friendship and assistance of some of America's skilled coin engravers through this interest in sulphides.

Small decorative pieces for use in jewelry settings are crafted in opal, opaque pink, blue, and green. The glass rods are being formed into designs approximately three-fourths of an inch in oval shapes for necklace drops or pins. Some of these glass rods are being drawn by Mr. Whittemore in his own shop. He can draw those that are one-eighth of an inch in diameter to a length of twenty feet, while those one-fourth of an inch in diameter can be drawn to a length of ten feet.

Recent Whittemore lamp-work paperweights include a pink flower against blue background. (Photograph by George J. Melvin.)

While Mr. Whittemore is still buying some of his tools, he has further extended his craftsmanship by manufacturing many of his own design. These include the pinch tools used to form leaves, a star-shaped mold, and clips similar to those used to hold the foot of a goblet while it is being formed. With completion of his own self-constructed furnace, Mr. Whittemore hopes to update his workshop equipment in readiness for his highly skilled paperweight production.

Francis and his wife Lois have four children, two sons and twin daughters. They live in Lansdale, Pennsylvania.

Part IV

Other
Contemporary American
Weight Makers

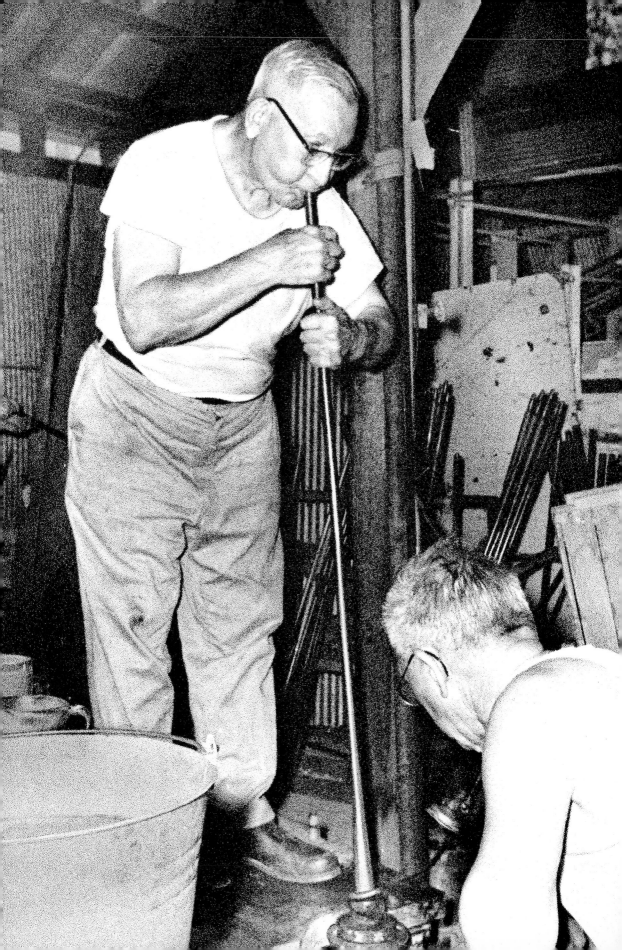

Chapter 26

The Dependent
Pot Workers

Each person one contacts who has a knowledge of weight makers seems to suggest a different craftsman's name. Sometimes these are men about whom research has been made—sometimes not. Information on the men mentioned in this chapter was gained either through visits to them or through correspondence.

Zack Boyd, Cambridge, Ohio

Zack Boyd, who was gaffer at Crystal Art Glass of Cambridge, Ohio, was a glass craftsman for many years, experienced through his varied work performed in twenty-six factories. He was one of the last of a generation of men who could truly be called a "Traveling Flint."

Born to Frank and Lovica Whissell Boyd on November 8, 1888, in Cambridge, Ohio, Zack started work at thirteen years of age, in June, 1902. The Cambridge Glass Company had been in production only since April, 1902.

Advanced from carry-in boy at sixty cents for nine hours' work to warm-in boy, to gatherer in 1906, he further advanced to "heavy gatherer," a job which required accurate gathers of crystal from molten pots to place in the molds of the heavy shop's largest-sized pressed-ware output. Although he could not remember all of his employers in his many years of experience in glass, Zack Boyd recalled working in these factories:

Ed Koztoski, the weight maker of Beacraft Glass Company, at work in Fort Smith, Arkansas. (Photograph courtesy of Edsel Ford.)

Zack Boyd "paddles" the ground color for the base of one of his paperweights. He crafted many paperweights at Crystal Art Glass, Cambridge, Ohio. (Photograph by George J. Melvin.)

1. Cambridge Glass Company until age twenty, with several return employments there.
2. Libbey Glass Company at Toledo, Ohio, where Zack gathered for their fine cut-glass bowls.
3. Lancaster, Ohio, a factory called by the workers "The Black Cat." It was actually the Hocking Glass Company (now Anchor-Hocking).
4. A return to Cambridge to work with Mike Metzger in lime glass (a new formula for blanks for pressing and cutting).
5. In 1917, to Imperial Glass Company, Inc. at Bellaire, Ohio, when Victor Wicke was president. Here he gathered for their heavy glass punch-bowl production. Zack worked at Imperial three different times.
6. After working at Cambridge Glass Company one turn, Zack took a street-car to Byesville, where he gathered for dental cuspidor output for a second turn daily.
7. Two different times Zack worked at Rodefer Glass Company in Bellaire, Ohio (now Rodefer-Gleason).

8. At East Palestine, Ohio, Zack was employed at John Kemple's factory making antique replica glass.

9. In Lancaster, Ohio, Zack worked at the "East End" and at

10. Lancaster Lens Factory.

11. In Brooklyn, New York, Zack worked at Gleason Teabout and at

12. DeMouth Glass Company.

13. At Viking Glass Company, New Martinsville, West Virginia, he was employed as a presser of large ware such as book ends and the like, and animals, including dogs, elephants, seals, and roosters.

14. St. Clair Glass Company at Ceredo, West Virginia, where auto headlight lenses were made.

15. Grossella at Clarksburg, West Virginia.

16. Master Glass Company at Bridgeport, Ohio.

17. Belmont Tumbler at Bellaire, Ohio, where he pressed goblets, tumblers, and trays.

18. Louie Glass Company at Weston, West Virginia.

19. West Virginia Specialty Glass Company of Weston, West Virginia.

20. Lornetta Glass on the Cheet River at Guyaux, Pennsylvania, near Point Marion, Pennsylvania.

21. Bieberthaler, Point Marion, Pennsylvania.

Elongated crystal, sapphire, and vaseline weights are designs of Zack Boyd. (Photograph by George J. Melvin.)

Zack Boyd enclosed miniature ceramic and sulphide animals, such as this rabbit, in bubbles with some paperweights. Also shown is a millefiori rod flower-design over white ground color. (Photograph by George J. Melvin.)

After retiring from glasswork in favor of two and a half years in civil service and later the management of National Hotel in Cambridge, Ohio, for three years, Mrs. Elizabeth Degenhart persuaded Zack to return to glass in September, 1964.

At Crystal Art Glass, Zack pressed ware in replica antique molds and made offhand items and many original designs of paperweights. Zack worked diligently at Crystal Art Glass and created many unusual paperweight designs for his employer, Mrs. Degenhart. Three of these she named "Peacock Feather," "Black Diamond," and "Millefiori." Zack made many weights also from the John Degenhart dies. Unusual colors, such as sapphire blue and vaseline, were used to create unique shapes of weights. Usually the colored glass was shaped into elongated flame forms with one large center bubble, or into large, almost ball-shaped weights in which were trapped many minute bubbles. These color weights were often further decorated with wheel cutting.

Boyd was married on May 10, 1907, to Erma Hollett. They had two children, a son, Bernard, who is a glass craftsman, and a daughter, Martha Dixon.

Zack died in September, 1968, after a very short illness.

Harry Caralluzzo, Toledo, Ohio

For many months I sought the whereabouts of Harry Caralluzzo, a contemporary glass craftsman of great skill. All reports of his work made me wish to interview him to get the story of how he crafts magnum-size, footed rose paperweights. All inquiries led me to the Vineland-Millville, New Jersey, area, but no one could actually supply the new address of a very recently removed Mr. Caralluzzo. Only a hint suggested he might have moved to Toledo, Ohio.

Once again, a good friend in glass research, a technical trouble-shooter for Pittsburgh Plate Glass Company, Jim Moss, came to my rescue and located one Harry Caralluzzo. Sure enough, he had moved to Toledo, Ohio, and is presently employed at Owens-Illinois. He is foreman of the hand-blown, hand-pressed department at the new-products development center there.

Harry Caralluzzo has worked in glasshouses for many years. Born to Frank and Mary Caralluzzo, January 10, 1923, in North Vineland, New

Harry Caralluzzo uses pucella to cut down rose paperweight. (Photograph by George J. Melvin.)

Jersey, Harry first started work with glass, at the age of fifteen, at August Hofbauer's factory in Vineland, New Jersey. An older brother, Sam, introduced Harry to glass manufacture.

At age eighteen, Harry transferred to Kimble Glass Company in Vineland, where he worked as a gatherer. This employment was interrupted by a twenty-seven-month service in the United States Army where Harry achieved the rank of Technical Sergeant.

Following Army duty, Harry was employed for a period of twenty years by Wheaton Glass Company at Millville, New Jersey. Here he became a journeyman on the I. S. machine under the Green Bottle Blowers Association. He also joined the American Flint Glass Workers' Union.

Shown a Ralph Barber footed rose paperweight, Harry was told that no one since Barber had made a satisfactory rose. This was his challenge. For a period of six years, Mr. Caralluzzo headed the hand-blown, hand-pressed-ware department at Wheaton Glass. During this time some off-hours were spent in the crafting of several sizes of footed rose paperweights. Brother Sam assisted Harry in this undertaking.

Designs crafted in paperweights include, in addition to roses, the morning glory, the poinsettia, threaded spirals, and bubble balls. Offhand creations include multicolor baskets, fish, vases, pitchers, perfume bottles, paperweight vases, ashtrays, candy dishes, and sugar and creamer sets.

Weights crafted by Harry Caralluzzo at Wheaton Glass Company, Millville, New Jersey, include a yellow morning glory over multicolor ground and a brilliant twelve-petal ruby-red footed rose with stamen and three dark green leaves. (Photograph by the author.)

Three magnum-size footed rose paperweights made by Harry Caralluzzo in pink with white-tipped petals, yellow, and deep red. The three green leaves are apple green in the pink weight and deep green in the others. (Photograph by George J. Melvin.)

Not all of Harry Caralluzzo's work is identifiable. He attempts to leave an "x" mark at the pontil break-off on the bottom of each paperweight. His earlier pieces were not so marked, but most of the later pieces show this mark rather distinctly.

Of his early rose paperweights made at Millville, New Jersey, Harry says, "I made some small blue roses about an inch in diameter, thirteen roses three and a half inches in diameter, and about twelve two and a half inches in diameter. Colors used for these roses were red, yellow, white, and burgundy."

Crimps used to make these roses varied also. A twelve-petal crimp was used to make the larger-size weight and a fifteen-petal crimp was used in the smaller weight. A seventeen-petal crimp creates a solid center in the rose. For colorants, Mr. Caralluzzo is using a supply of 150 pounds of cullet from the Durand Glass Company.

One collector who encouraged Harry in his attempt to craft footed rose paperweights has a large collection of Caralluzzo work. This collection is a very interesting study in the increasing skill shown in crafting this product—from the irregular early output to a final trio of perfectly beautiful footed rose paperweights which would rate tops in any collection.

Work at Owens-Illinois in the new-products development center allows little time for offhand crafting of glass since off-hour work is not permitted in this factory. In fact, Harry can count only nine successful Millville-type roses since leaving the Wheaton plant. He crafted beautiful red and yellow roses at the glass factory of a friend for a brief period in 1968. Some of these are twenty-one petal roses.

Mr. Caralluzzo is a large, well-built man. He talks with justifiable pride about his craftsmanship, explaining earnestly and patiently to a novice like me how each piece of his glass is created. His family includes a very pleasant wife, Martha, a daughter, Christine, and a son, Harry Junior.

William E. Claytor, Hartford City, Indiana

William E. Claytor, who was born in December, 1885, spent his life working in glasshouses as an iron- and paste-mold blower—most of the work having been done for the Sneath Glass Company in Hartford City, Indiana. At this factory he was permitted to make paperweights during the weekends. Mr. Claytor retired from plant work in 1952.

Following World War II, Mr. Claytor and his son built a backyard shop at 1001 North Jefferson Street, Hartford City, Indiana, for the purpose of novelty glass manufacture. Here they turned out paperweights, but found it difficult to comply with the price requests of jobbers and wholesale men. This fact caused the Claytors to reduce production to about two or three tanks of glass run each winter.

Three types of paperweights crafted by William E. Claytor: A plaque name weight, a multicolor fragment design, and a three-lily weight. (Photograph by George J. Melvin.)

Paperweight designs, offhand vases made by John Di Bella, formerly of Catlettsburg, Kentucky. (Photographs by the author.)

While the furnace, tools, and ability are still available at Claytor's, no weights are being produced today. Weights made previously included lily designs, decal, and name weights.

John Di Bella, Catlettsburg, Kentucky

John Di Bella, son of an Italian glass-plant manager, gained training as a glassworker before coming to the United States from Sicily. He was just twelve years of age when he left his native land. Working in various United States glass plants, he gained much knowledge of glass production. John's knowledge of the chemistry of glass was acquired through his trial-and-error experimentations of many years. Hard work and honest labor finally gained him ownership of his own glass plant. His last plant was located at Catlettsburg, Kentucky, where he started production in a factory, largely self-planned and self-constructed. John's skills included building his own glass furnace with proper connections, etc.

His products included many speciality handmade pieces such as paperweights, blown vases, sugars and creamers, ashtrays, three sizes of kerosene oil lamps with crimped shades to match, cruets, tumblers, and water pitchers.

John Di Bella died on October 9, 1963. His wife Ethel and a son, Jack, are living at the site of the small glass plant, which has stood idle since his death. His widow explained that when the factory was in production, two furnaces containing four pots each were in use. From these pots John Di Bella's greatest production was either antique lamps or off-hand novelty ware.

An item of interest was the paperweight flower vase. The design of the heavy bottom portion formed a paperweight to which a blown vase was added. The weight portion of the vase might be designed with either an arrangement of air-trap bubbles or a colored flower made by using powdered glass in a die form. On some examples of this vase crystal was applied in the form of a decorated fluting or leaf-and-stem motif spiralling up the sides of the vase. In other examples colored glass was used.

Few of Di Bella's paperweights were to be seen at the factory as most had been sent out to prospective purchasers as samples. One paperweight I saw contained a red powdered glass die design reading "God Bless America." A small flag centered this design.

Frank J. Hamilton, Star City, West Virginia

A new star in paperweight manufacture appeared on the horizon when, in 1963, John Gentile started to train his grandson, Frank J. Hamilton, in the crafting of production paperweights.

Born April 5, 1950, to Harold and Phoebe Mae Hamilton, Frank had an opportunity, throughout much of his young life, to watch how glass was crafted. While in high school, he joined his grandfather as a carry-in boy or in any other general factory part-time capacity. As soon as he was of legal age to handle hot glass, he started in earnest to craft the many production-weight designs at the Gentile Glass Company under the careful tutelage of both grandmother Gertrude and grandfather John Gentile.

Upon completion of his high-school education, Frank began full-time employment and soon acquired a fine skill in crafting paperweights and doorstops. On the Gentile gift-counter shelves, only Frank and his grandmother can accurately determine which weights are made by Frank and which are by John Gentile.

Frank Hamilton of Gentile Glass Company. (Photograph by George J. Melvin.)

An example of Frank Hamilton's abstract sculpture. (Photograph by the author.)

He has successfully experimented with modern free-form glass paperweights and many of the well-known die and bubble designs usually made at Gentile's factory, all pictured in this text. He has also crafted a multicolor swirled pencil holder and very popular multicolor abstract paperweights.

Frank is a young craftsman of great promise. He is one of the few young American glassmakers devoting full time to acquiring expert skill in weight making. Much of America's future in pot-type paperweights rests with Frank Hamilton.

Frank Hamilton's abstract magnum weights are made in a variety of color combinations and are very popular. This one is red, white, and blue. (Photograph by the author.)

James G. Hamilton, Star City, West Virginia

James G. Hamilton, born March 15, 1936, at Booth, West Virginia, entered the glass trade after completion of Army duty in 1957. He has acquired much skill as a glass cutter and engraver and manages the glass-cutting and decorating department of his stepfather's Gentile Glass Company. Jimmy does all the facet cutting on Gentile's collectors' weights.

During off-hours from his regular job of faceting paperweights and decorating glass, Jimmy will frequently pick up a pontil to craft paperweights. He is familiar with all the paperweight processes and has made several types of production weights including spirals, mottoes, fruit, five-flower, double-bubble, broken cane, and a few others of odd designs. He signs his weights with a J. H. die, which helps the collector distinguish his from others made at the Gentile factory.

James Hamilton at a wheel decorating glass blanks which are manufactured at several different factories. This type of work is practiced by a decreasing number of craftsmen as machine decorating replaces hand work in many shops. (Photograph by George J. Melvin.)

Jimmy Hamilton sometimes crafts weights in free time from his regular job of faceting paperweights and decorating glass. He signs his weights with a J.H. die to distinguish his from others made at the Gentile factory. (Photograph by the author.)

While it is good that Jimmy Hamilton can and does make occasional paperweights, his real contribution to the glass world is his skill in faceting the many beautiful Gentile designs for the collectors' market.

Edward Koztoski, Fort Smith, Arkansas

A reply to an inquiry to the Fort Smith Chamber of Commerce revealed that there is a glass manufacturing plant in Fort Smith, Arkansas, which makes paperweights—the factory of Alvin Beacraft—known as the Beacraft Glass Company.

Five men are employed at this one-story, one-room glasshouse from 6 A.M. to 2:45 P.M. daily. Using old glass bottles and jars and some purchased colors and ingredients, these men presently put out many blown novelties. The colors are sandwiched between crystal layers of glass. One worker, Edward Koztoski, a native of Poland, born March 5, 1889, makes Beacraft's paperweights. Those I have seen include two sizes of glass swirls, which are dropped into a dome-shaped mold and cut off. These are made in such color combinations as blue and white; green, pink, and white; and orange, brown, and white. Also, there is a larger bottle-green glass weight with multicolor flowers centered with air bubbles, made by inserting an ice pick. I own two Beacraft weights. One has five flowers over a white base color. Air bubbles center each flower, and one air bubble is spaced between each of the four flowers on the perimenter. This weight has been rough-ground only at the pontil. The other weight has a small white mushroom-type base, one large multicolored glass-fragment flower with a center bubble, and four perimeter bubbles. No grinding was done at the cutoff of this weight, and skilled blocking with a resulting perfect shaping is apparent at the pontil breakoff. Another Beacraft weight is shaped like a small chicken. Beacraft weights are for sale at antique fairs in the eastern United States, indicating that they do get far from Arkansas.

Roberto Moretti, Ceredo, West Virginia

The Pilgrim Glass Corporation, Pilgrim Valley, Ceredo, West Virginia, is currently making handcrafted paperweights. Those manufactured are an elephant, a donkey, three sizes of a whale, two sizes of a swan, horses, fish, cats, birds, turtles, etc. Some of these are made in frosted crystal, while others are crafted in various colors including sky blue, topaz, avocado, amethyst, and tangerine. Another type of Pilgrim weight is the large bubble weight. Many rows of minute bubbles are trapped in a colored glass which is finally cased in crystal to make a standard-size weight. Some of these weights have one large center bubble.

Paperweights made by Edward Koztoski at the Beacraft Glass Company. *Left to right:* Large flower of multicolored bits cased with green tinted glass; blue-and-white swirl-mold pressed weight; green, white, orange, and brown colors swirled into press mold; footed chicken form; five multicolored flowers over white base, cased with pale green tinted glass. (Photograph by George J. Melvin.)

Roberto Moretti cuts down a paperweight at his bench in factory of the Pilgrim Glass Corporation, Ceredo, West Virginia. (Photograph by the author.)

A very descriptive letter from Mr. Alfred E. Knobler, president of the Pilgrim Glass Corporation, follows: "Our paperweights are made completely by hand and are the work of the most skilled of our glassworkers. In most cases these men work alone or sometimes in small teams of two or three men. The work is painstakingly slow, and we can only produce five or six pieces per hour."

Looking over a recent catalog from Pilgrim Glass Corporation, I noted several pages of interesting glass animals and birds, large and small, some cased, some acid etched, some sculptured. All of these could be a nucleus for a fascinating paperweight collection because these novel objects may be used either as paperweights or for decoration.

Another section of the catalog revealed a much greater variety of bubble and blown paperweights than I reported in the first edition of *American Glass Paperweights and Their Makers.* Included in the new designs are a carnation in red, blue, topaz, or white, a Millville rose in red, and swirl and bubble weights with diamond facets. All of these designs indicate a new interest in crafting paperweights at Pilgrim and most certainly that highly skilled craftsmen are at work there. The answer lies with Roberto Moretti, his brother Alessandro, and his brother-in-law Mario Sandon.

While paperweights and other production art-glass items crafted at Pilgrim are Roberto's livelihood, his heart has been won by after-hour glass sculpture created from hot glass. His widely acclaimed glass sculptures prove his love for this work. Moretti won first prize at the Greater Huntington Arts Festival in October 1968 for his glass sculptured piece entitled "Sorrow" and was honored to have his "Glass Nativity" shown for a month at the Corning Museum of Glass in December 1968.

Paul N. Perrot, Director of the Corning Museum, said of this exhibit:

> Sculpture in glass is entirely different from sculpture in any other material. Other substances rely for their effect on reflected light while glass combines both reflected and transmitted light. This, added to a high index of refraction and consequent inner reflections of glass, creates visual effects which, in the hands of a talented artist, can produce highly evocative and decorative results.

Roberto Moretti crafted this footed blue-and-white carnation paperweight. (Photograph by the author.)

Mr. Moretti's stylized shapes reveal a complete understanding of the fluid properties of glass and the subtle harmonies which can be achieved by understanding its inner light. His work, as some of his colleagues' in Italy and in the United States, demonstrates that in skillful hands glass is a sculptural medium and that particularly happy results can be achieved when both the originator of the design and its executor are linked in one person.

While many of the craftsmen reported in this book are descended from fine European glassworkers, Roberto Moretti is the first glass artist I have found to have come directly from Italy in recent years. Descended from Morettis who worked in glass as early as the seventeenth century, this highly skilled artist came to the United States in 1956. He was born in Murano, Italy, September 16, 1930, to Adalgisa and Umberto Moretti. At age thirteen, he started to work in glass in Murano, where he progressed from third, to second, to first helper, and to finisher. He learned the basic skills of glassblowing and the skill of carving.

Only in 1965 did Roberto explore glass as a sculptural medium. Using the usual simple glassworker's tools, such as pucella, shears, and palette-type knife, he has learned to coax hot glass into shapes pleasing to himself and, judging from acclaim, pleasing to the public. These forms, beautiful for their simplicity—the understatements of the human figure—evolved after much soul searching. Initial attempts and experimentation in creating the human figure after the classical ideals of the Greeks and Romans left Roberto unhappy with what he felt were inadequate results. As he learned to let his medium dictate somewhat the outcome of his sculptured ideas, predetermined by sketches, his sculptures matured into true creativity.

Great determination and skill must combine to create from the fast-cooling fluid glass an artisan's vision of beauty—a message to the viewer. This combination Roberto Moretti possesses.

John D. Murphy, Cameron, West Virginia

Traditionally the first two weeks in July are vacation weeks at all the Ohio Valley glasshouses and factories. This is a period when glass craftsmen take a "busman's holiday" and travel far and wide talking with or, where possible, viewing other craftsmen at work.

John Murphy completes a weight by cutting down the glass gather in a revolving motion along the sharp edge of the presser's kettle plate. (Photograph by the author.)

Early in July, 1969, a young craftsman, John D. Murphy, put his box of newly crafted paperweights in his car and made a straight way (if that is possible on the mountainous roads of West Virginia) to Star City to confer with John Gentile. He sought help in making pot-type paperweights. Luckily for me, I arrived at Gentile's only a few minutes after.

John Murphy is working in the old tradition—during off-hours—from the pots of excellent crystal at the Fostoria Glass Company, Moundsville, West Virginia, where he is a presser. Pre-work hours and noon-hour breaks permit time for weight making.

Unusual methods of weight manufacture and the type of colorants used make Murphy's weight production unique today. Colorants used are bits of glass cullet picked up from the waste piles of the many glass factories he visits; for example, his blue is milk of magnesia bottle bits. This practice is good in that these bits of glass are formed, without dies, into most original flowers, swirls, and base colors to make quite different-appearing designs. On the other hand, it is not so good in that many glass colorants picked up for use are not compatible with the sparkling crystal of the Fostoria pots. This results in a higher percentage of fractures in weights than is desirable.

Even more miraculous is that this young craftsman is working with only a pontil—no blocking tools and no dies, with the exception of three experimental designs he carved in a carbon block. His crystal gather is rotated on his pontil until the glass, by gravity flow, takes on the shape desired—amazingly even and true.

Watching John Murphy make a weight is most interesting. Thanks to David Dalzell, Jr., of Fostoria Glass Company, I was permitted to go onto the factory floor and make photographs of the process.

Without benefit of marver, the initial gather of crystal is rotated on the end of the pontil. When a desired form is achieved, the pontil is upended to pick up prearranged colored bits of glass from a metal tray of a glass-pressing machine. A quick trip to the glory hole, where the bits are warmed-in, prepares the weight for the ice-pick pierces to make air traps as flower centers. A second and final crystal gather is rotated on the pontil. To accomplish a cut-down, ordinarily performed with a pucella, John rotates his pontil along the sharp edge of the kettle plate. Skillfully rotating his pontil, the weight is at one time formed and the glass gather reduced at the tip of the pontil to permit a completed weight to be struck off onto the moving table of the lehr for annealing. I felt as I watched John Murphy that he was reviving the art of weight making as it must have been practiced at the turn of the century by some of the glassworkers in the then-numerous Ohio Valley glasshouses, even though I never had seen this process nor had it described to me.

John is a man of few words. He observes much. His experimentation at Fostoria has been closely observed by his colleagues, eight of whom have joined him in weight making. They are Jack Wayne, Sam Lennox, Kenny Robinson, Jim Williamson, Freddy Wilkerson, Fount Myers, Clarence Johnson, and Ray Lohr. They have persuaded B. N. Suter in the Fostoria shop to facet some of their designs.

Many glasshouses of this era do not permit their employees the off-hour privilege of whimsy glass crafting. It is refreshing and encouraging to find that Fostoria Glass Company values the creative spirit of their employees. The zest of these workmen for their regular jobs was evident. Perhaps Fostoria, in permitting off-hour creativity, is adding much to good employee relationships.

John David Murphy was born March 7, 1938, a son of John Edward and Gay Lively Murphy. He attended the public schools of Cameron, West Virginia, but dropped out of high school. He first worked with a construction firm, before his employment at Fostoria.

John is an amateur artist. His subjects include landscapes and objects from nature. From his cigarette-lighter he copied a painting on a piece of opal glass. This fisherman sketch was cased in crystal—but unfortunately the weight fractured. The weight was partially saved by careful grinding.

In viewing in past years the products of other glass craftsmen, John decided he liked the looks of paperweights. To satisfy his curiosity about how they were made, he undertook to turn these out in his own way without benefit of teacher or research. Naturally the output described is limited. This young craftsman is consumed with a desire, a will, and a drive to make good paperweights. It is hoped his desire may blossom into full fruit.

Patrick Naples, Clayton, New Jersey

While I was on a brief vacation trip to South Jersey, interested paperweight collectors mentioned a name I had not previously heard—that of Patrick Naples.

As in most cases with glassworkers in South Jersey, this craftsman has moved about frequently in his employment. First employed at Vineland, New Jersey, as a fifteen-year-old lad in the Kimble Glass Company, Pat saw paperweights crafted during noon-hour lunch-breaks by older men. This was in the days when such experimental work was done with the company's permission.

At Kimble Glass, Pat gained the friendship of William Vallo who carefully tutored him in glass craftsmanship. In 1948, Mr. Vallo moved to Doerr Glass Company, of Vineland, New Jersey, young Pat following along.

Pat Naples at the gaffer's bench of Bob Dobson's Iona Glass Works, Iona, New Jersey. (Photograph courtesy of Roy C. Horner.)

In 1953, Pat—who is the son of Mike, a bricklayer, and his wife Rose Naples—decided to try his hand at his father's trade. This he followed until 1957. In 1958 he married Doris Roun and moved to Clayton, New Jersey, where he was employed by Ollie Clevenger at the Clevenger Brothers Glass Works.

Returning to Kimble Glass Company in 1960, Pat Naples created some of his finest offhand pieces until 1965. The Clevenger plant, under the management of Mr. J. Travis, offered Pat many opportunities if he would return there. Persuading Mr. Vallo and the "grand old man of South Jersey Glass"—Gus Hofbauer—to join him, many of Clevenger's offhand and mold items were re-created for an ever-enlarging trade. This employment was short.

By the time that Doerr Glass reopened in late 1965, both Mr. Vallo and Pat Naples returned to glasswork there—Pat to create his first rose paperweight. Since Mr. Vallo had worked with Ralph Barber and had created roses as late as 1939, he agreed to permit Pat to use existing crimps and to teach him the art of "Millville" or "Jersey" rose paperweight making.

Pat Naples creates rose designs with fourteen, fifteen, eighteen, or twenty-one petals in red, yellow, blue, white, orange, lavender, and pink. Some are red with white-tipped petals, blue with white-tipped petals, and white with blue-tipped petals. Other paperweight designs crafted by this artisan include butterflies, a variety of flower designs, animals, nameplate weights, and bubble weights.

Peter Knapp Raymond, Williamstown, West Virginia

Now retired, glassworker Peter K. Raymond lives at Williamstown, West Virginia.

Born November 16, 1886, Mr. Raymond was introduced to glasswork at an early age, having worked at the old Jefferson Glass Company at Steubenville, Ohio. One of his teachers, John Q. Shaffer, asked Peter to help him make paperweights. This experience was the foundation for

A footed red rose made by Pat Naples. (Photograph by the author.)

weight making which Mr. Raymond started about 1910. After first trying to make weights with names in them, it was not long until all types of flowers were created by Mr. Raymond using many glass colorants.

In later years while employed by the Fenton Art Glass Company, Williamstown, West Virginia, Mr. Raymond was permitted to make weights at hours when the company was not in production. The largest weight he created was a doorstop weighing 11 pounds 4 ounces, which is now in the office of the Fenton Art Glass Company, Williamstown, West Virginia.

Mr. Raymond says, "It is true that I made thousands of weights, but I do not have a good one for myself today." The weights he made at Fenton were sold as rapidly as they were produced.

The weight shown on this page is a design different from the weights of other craftsmen I contacted. It is a large single pink-and-white, four-petal, day-lily-type flower centered with four red cane stamens. At the base of the flower are four green leaves. The design is quite attractive. This was also made in blue.

Other weights which Mr. Raymond displayed were his early six-petal (made of canes) flower and a beautiful weight designed later containing six yellow canes formed into a day-lily-type flower with three stamens over a multicolored base. Mr. Raymond says that this was referred to by craftsmen as the Star weight.

Like other craftsmen, Peter Raymond tried making the magnum footed rose weight. He has at his home two experimental rose paperweights. One contains eleven pink petals, the other twelve petals made with a crimp.

Four-petal pink lily with red cane stamen, four green leaves, made by Peter K. Raymond. (Photograph by the author.)

Peter K. Raymond weights. Six-cane flower weights in rose and yellow. Note the footed rose weights. (Photograph by George J. Melvin.)

Four green leaves complete this model. In *The Fenton Story of Glass Making,* his work is praised:

> Pete Raymond, who made glass the first day the factory operated, came to Williamstown to visit during the Christmas holidays in 1906 and stayed to work at the plant more than half a century. During his tenure he fulfilled most of the skilled jobs in the glassworks. He made one of his most important contributions while working as a glass finisher on tumblers. One day, purely as an experiment, he reheated the rim of a tumbler and spun a delicate ring of blue glass to the edge. This dazzling piece of glassware was the forerunner of Fenton's exclusive Peach Crest and Silver Crest ware. The process of adding the distinctive crystal edge to fine pieces has remained a secret of Fenton craftsmen since the day Raymond developed the technique.

The Fenton Story of Glass Making, as told by Alan Linn. Used by special permission.

A striped-rod star weight by Peter Raymond. (Photograph by the author.)

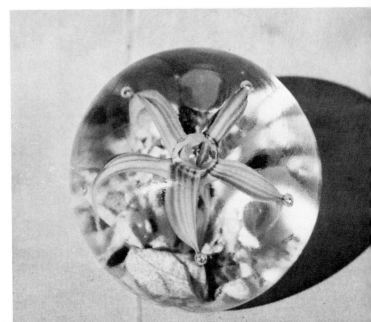

Ralph Rousseau, Morgantown, West Virginia

A regularly employed gatherer at the Seneca Glass Company, Morgantown, West Virginia, is Ralph Rousseau. During off-hours Mr. Rousseau experimented for about one and a half years in the manufacture of glass paperweights. In 1968 Seneca curtailed this privilege.

Born on February 20, 1900, Ralph Rousseau entered the Seneca Glass factory at the age of ten. He worked then as a carry-in boy. Though he spent twenty-three years as a coal miner, Mr. Rousseau never gave up a liking for glass manufacture. At various times he has been employed in glass factories at Cameron, West Virginia; the McDonald Tumbler Company, McDonald, Pennsylvania; Paden City Glass Company, Paden City, West Virginia; Bartlett-Collins at Sapulpa, Oklahoma; and other factories located in Ohio, California, and West Virginia. Ralph Rousseau says, "I was truly a 'Traveling Flint.' "

Prior to 1916 when machinery took over the window-glass production, Ralph Rousseau was employed as window-glass craftsman. He explained that it was common practice to swing glass gathers weighing 26 to 45

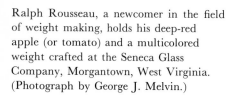

Ralph Rousseau, a newcomer in the field of weight making, holds his deep-red apple (or tomato) and a multicolored weight crafted at the Seneca Glass Company, Morgantown, West Virginia. (Photograph by George J. Melvin.)

A "Dutch" Sommers weight in the collection of James Moss. The design is a large mushroom or swirl cased with green glass. An Alex Stelzer weight made of canes representing a four-petal flower, each petal containing one transparent red center cane surrounded by two opaque pale blue-green canes and two opaque outer canes of pale yellow-green. Four short red canes separate the four flower petals. Base color is very pale yellow-green pierced with pinpoint bubbles. (Photographs by George J. Melvin.)

pounds from a pipe in the window-glass process. He believes that this method of production has become almost a lost art.

This weight craftsman came to my attention when he called at the Gentile Glass Company to show his teacher, John Gentile, the products of his latest efforts in weight design. Rousseau carried a small box containing six red apples. These he had blown of lead crystal from Seneca pots, flashed, and then cased again with crystal. A crystal bit was added to form a stem. These tomato-shaped weights would have been finished as tomatoes, not apples, had the necessary green glass been available for the stems.

"Dutch" Sommers and Alex Stelzer, Toledo, Ohio

Some collectors recall the names of "Dutch" Sommers of Toledo, Ohio, and Alex Stelzer, a Czechoslovakian who made weights about thirty years ago at Libbey Glass Company in Toledo. Mr. Al G. Smith, Press Relations Manager at Owens-Illinois, was very helpful in verifying that these men worked at Libbey Glass Company. His letter is quoted:

"George Sommers went to work at the Libbey Glass Company plant here in 1905 at the age of fifteen. Old pictures of him in the files of the Libbey Plant show him blowing glass tableware in our old Factory A (the old hand factory at Libbey). His job was a 'Paste Mold Gatherer.' A Libbey employee comments that he must have been very good because of the pictures of him in the files.

"Alexander Stelzer went to work at Libbey in 1907. He remained with the Company until December 3, 1948, at which time Libbey discontinued making handblown glass. His last job was furnace and tank supervisor.

"As far as I have been able to learn, Libbey Glass Company never made paperweights for sale. However, glass blowers at the Libbey factory were allowed to make paperweights and other glass articles on their own time. The workers gave these away to friends or sold them and these, I think, are the paperweights now in circulation."

In my research I have found more paperweights attributed to Alex Stelzer than to Dutch Sommers. This could be due, in part, to the fact that Alex Stelzer and Arthur Gorham were friends. Mr. Gorham purchased for resale many Stelzer weights.

Jonathan R. Stone, Caney, Kansas

Another glassworker, Jonathan R. Stone, born near Portland, Jay County, Indiana, April 15, 1898, started to work in glasshouses when he was fourteen. Stone's experience includes work at MacBeth-Evans, Elwood, Indiana, and New Cumberland and Huntington, West Virginia. He also worked at the Radiant Factory, Fort Smith, Arkansas, and Texas Glass Factory at Brownwood, Texas.

The Texas factory is owned by Clyde Graham, a longtime friend of Stone's and an associate when both worked at Fort Smith, Arkansas. Graham had, in his earlier days, worked with Ralph Barber at Millville, New Jersey. Ray Stone is adept at encasing nameplates in weights and still makes a few of these and the lily designs each year. As of October, 1964, he joined his son, L. E. Stone, at Caney, Kansas, in the Continental Glass Manufacturers, Incorporated, to manufacture glass chimneys and glass novelties.

Jonathan R. Stone weights. *Left to right:* Greentown caramel fragments with a large center bubble; Greentown caramel fragments enclosed in a pencil-holder weight; swirl pen holder; vase made of opaque white, cased with emerald green; Fowlerton-type weight made with pale canary yellow glass over Greentown fragments; ivy bowl of pale canary glass over Greentown caramel fragments. (Photograph by George J. Melvin.)

A recent J. R. Stone weight encloses a decal of Christ's head. (Photograph by the author.)

Misfortune overtook the new firm of Continental Glass Manufacturers, Incorporated, when after three brief months of operation the plant was forced to close down due to the illness of L. E. Stone. In the brief period the firm was in operation, J. R. Stone made some interesting Fowlerton, Indiana, replica paperweights and taught his grandson to make weights. Fortunately, a portion of the production at the Caney, Kansas, plant is clearly identified by a die bearing the plant name. This was applied to the pontil end of the pieces while the glass was still molten.

At Mr. Stone's home in Goldsmith, Indiana, I saw some of his glass products—a Kokomo green-and-white overlay vase, lily-design pen holders, Greentown caramel-fragment pencil holders, and decal weights.

Charles B. Windsor, Jr., Milton, West Virginia

When researching glass craftsmen for the first edition of this book the author made visits to many glasshouses in search of paperweight craftsmen. Many factories had neither paperweights nor craftsmen to report at that time.

At Blenko Glass Company, Charles B. Windsor, Jr., crafts paperweights marketed by the firm. (Photograph by the author.)

Recent research for this new edition produced a vastly different story. At every factory visited some form of paperweight was offered for sale in the display rooms.

At Blenko Glass Company, Incorporated, Milton, West Virginia, fine paperweights are currently made on a production basis. Inquiry revealed that these are crafted exclusively by Charles B. Windsor, Jr. Except for three years spent in Army service (1943–1946), Mr. Windsor has been at Blenko ever since his first employment there August 15, 1942. During his wartime service in Europe he first became interested in paperweights.

Experimenting during off-hours Charles Windsor learned to make paperweights soon after his return in 1946. He created a variety of designs but many proved too difficult to mass produce. While Blenko did manufacture weights some thirty years ago, the venture did not prove popular enough to continue—so was curtailed after about one year.

In 1968 the designer for Blenko, J. P. Myers, suggested that paperweights again be produced. Since Mr. Windsor was the only employee who had knowledge of and experience in making paperweights, this production fell to him. From his earlier experiments he selected designs which he felt could be mass produced. These include a yellow spiral sphere, a knob-topped, air-twist around a tangerine center cylinder, an air-twist sphere in olive, a blue centered sphere with elongated perimeter air traps, and an inverted top-shaped weight with air twists around a blue center. All of these weights are approximately $3\frac{3}{4}$ inches in diameter or magnum in size. Turquoise and olive have proved to be the most popular colors.

While Charles Windsor's father and three uncles were at times employed in the glass industry, only one uncle stayed long enough to retire from Owens-Illinois Glass Company.

Charles B. and Lona F. Windsor are the parents of Charles, Jr., who was born in Handley, West Virginia, on October 12, 1924. He was graduated from high school and the Army communication school. He studied one semester at Marshall University prior to entering the field of glass manufacture.

William Zick; Emil Kuhn, Morgantown, West Virginia

In the earlier days of glass manufacture in the Pittsburgh and Wheeling area plants, the glassworker spent off-hours making weights from the firm's crystal pots. As market conditions developed into keener competition between factories and countries, this practice was limited in many factories. However, there are some plants in which weights may still be made by employees. Those I know of include the Rodefer-Gleason Glass Company, Bellaire, Ohio, and the Morgantown Glassware Guild, Incorporated, Morgantown, West Virginia, where William Zick, Sr., followed by William Zick, Jr., Emil Kuhn, and others made weights.

William Zick, Sr., started to work at old "Economy" in Morgantown, West Virginia, in 1904. When the name was changed to the Morgantown Glassware Guild, Incorporated, he remained as an employee, retiring in 1953 at the age of eighty. His weights were the products of lunch-hour or after-hours work.

William Zick, Jr., born November 26, 1908, started to work at the Morgantown Glassware Guild, Incorporated, when he was seventeen years of age. This large glasshouse with its two hundred employees working from eighteen pots afforded experience in all lines of glass manufacture. Today Bill Zick is a foreman, and this responsibility allows him little time for weight making. Sometimes on Fridays, after other workers have left, Bill makes about eight to ten paperweights. His designs include a butterfly and more recently a silk-screened image of the late President John F. Kennedy encased in crystal. Emil Kuhn formerly made weights at the Morgantown Guild but has not made any for about eight years.

Weights made at the Morgantown Glassware Guild, Incorporated, by Emil Kuhn and William Zick, Sr. *Left to right:* Opaque white with black crimped design, made by Kuhn; pale turquoise three-petal flower over light-blue and silver particle base, made by Zick; yellow single flower over cobalt and silver bit base color, made by Zick. (Photograph by George J. Melvin.)

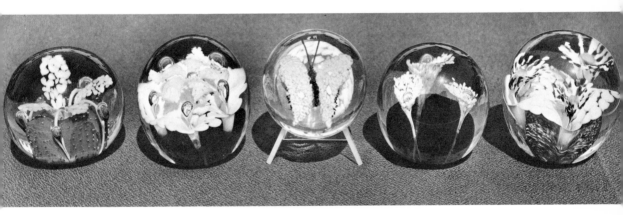

Weights made at the Morgantown Glassware Guild, Incorporated, by William Zick, Jr. *Left to right:* Four-petal white flower over red base, pierced with minute bubbles; five-petal pale blue flower over milk white and cobalt blue base layers; yellow butterfly, black body over blue base color; three white lily flowers over deep cobalt-blue base; three rose-and-white lily flowers over opaque red-and-white base. (Photograph by George J. Melvin.)

Part V

Paperweight Variations

Chapter 27

Paperweight
Variations

Many paperweight fanciers restrict their collections to paperweights as such, while other collectors enjoy the many variations crafted in some of the American glass shops and factories. Some of these unique pieces have been mentioned in the discussion of the individual craftsman. However, I believe these production variations are worthy of special note here.

As previously reported, doorstops and paperweight lamps have found favor in many homes as decorative as well as utilitarian objects. To this list has been added a surprising number of old and contemporary products crafted by means of a paperweight technique. It is recorded here so that perhaps this may open a new avenue of collecting or a pleasurable hobby for some.

Doorstops

Since paperweight craftsmen—that is, the pot or furnace workers—in the past and to a limited degree today do make doorstops, some mention of doorstops is necessary.

A doorstop is an oversized paperweight, heavier and larger in height and diameter. Very often designs similar to those used in paperweights are incorporated in the doorstops; on the other hand, some craftsmen's specials show the evidence of careful planning and execution of very ingenious and intricate designs.

A shop at the Rodefer-Gleason Glass Company, Bellaire, Ohio, pressing dental trays. Their famous "float" paperweights are very infrequently run in contemporary times. (Photograph by George J. Melvin.)

Paperweight lamps are a true collector's item because so few are made today. Shown are examples of lamps created with parts manufactured by (*Left*) John Degenhart, (*Center*) St. Clair Glass Works and (*Right*) Zimmerman Art Glass Company. Note that Zimmerman crafted a base for his lamp.

The child's unfortunate practice (or game) of shooting marbles at a doorstop marred many pieces that would have otherwise borne only the marks of their intended use through time.

Contemporary weightmakers who produce doorstops to order are Gentile and Zimmerman. Doorstops were formerly made by St. Clair, Rithner, and the Degenharts.

Paperweight Lamps

Another product both beautiful and collectable, which has been manufactured by paperweight craftsmen, is a wide variety in size and color of table lamps. Five craftsmen are known to have created lamps in recent years: Degenhart, Gentile, St. Clair, Stone, and Zimmerman.

Paperweight lamps are frequently assembled with a prefabricated plain or faceted crystal base together with brass risers to separate the decorative glass balls created by the individual craftsman. Some makers topped their lamps with a handmade glass finial. Each weightmaker will declare that lamp parts are heavy to handle in manufacture, difficult to anneal properly, and trying to assemble attractively. For these reasons no craftsman is presently manufacturing lamp parts in quantity. Collectors who possess paperweight-type glass lamps should be appreciative of their beauty and aware of their value which will undoubtedly appreciate rapidly.

Illustrated are three lamps, each made by a different craftsman.

1. John Degenhart—lily-type multicolor flowers in two differently shaped parts.
2. Peter Gentile created a ruby spiral, five-flower red-and-white section, and a crystal bubble ball. These three sizes and three varying shapes make an interesting lamp.
3. St. Clair Glass Works—three-part lamp showing five white lilies over emerald green in each part.
4. Jonathan R. Stone used two-tone Greentown, Indiana, caramel-glass fragments for lily-type flowers in three sizes and three shapes of lamp parts. Rare.
5. Zimmerman Art Glass Company made a lamp complete with hand-crafted base and finial. Cobalt flowers are cased in crystal balls in the example illustrated.

Steuben Glass

A contemporary weight of crystal beauty is the eight-cane, spiral paperweight with one large center bubble which is made at the Steuben Glass Plant in Corning, New York. Many other designs made by Steuben Glass could be used as paperweights. The crystal in Steuben products is of the most desirable sparkling purity and beauty.

A well-known and much appreciated contemporary glass factory, particularly from the collector's point of view, is Steuben Glass at Corning, New York. A skillful blending of management and production has concentrated on the trilogy of material, workmanship, and design to produce the most renowned of United States glass objects.

The following quote is from the book *The Story of Steuben Glass:* "To create forms that would reveal the crystal's essential qualities of transparency, brilliance, and colorlessness early became the guiding principle of Steuben."

Two works which exemplify this principle are paperweight productions called: (1) the Spiral and (2) the Star Crystal.

Proud is the collector who can add these paperweights to his treasured display.

Mr. Kenneth Wilson of Corning Museum supplied me with the names of two men who did make some contemporary weights at Corning, New York. They are Paul A. Holton of Corning and Leonard Parker of Lawrenceville, Pennsylvania. Weights were made not as Steuben products, so none were ever signed or marketed. They were created as gifts to shopboys, friends, and neighbors.

Mr. Holton's reply to my inquiry about these colorful weights revealed company policy no longer permits this practice. The second reason is that the lunch period has been reduced to twenty minutes from an hour when offhand weights could be made.

Mr. Holton revealed that in his forty-three years as a glassworker with Corning and Steuben works, workers at different times made glass canes, letter openers, stocking darners, and cigarette and cigar holders. Only around Christmas did they make paperweights. From older glassworkers, Samuel Bunell, Joseph Sponer, and Nels Pierson (all workers under Frederick Carder), modern Steuben workers—Paul A. Holton, Leonard Parker, Blair Hardenberg—learned to make paperweights and other offhand glasswork years ago when they were shopboys. Most of these men made only about twenty-five weights. Mr. Holton, however, made between seventy-five and one hundred paperweights in a gold ruby flower, as well as green, amethyst, yellow, dark purple, white, and blue five-petal flowers plus five rose paperweights. These weights vary in size from three inches to grapefruit size. Variations in design include weights containing two

Paperweights made at the Pilgrim Glass Corporation, Ceredo, West Virginia. (Photograph courtesy of the Pilgrim Glass Corporation.)

Crystal paperweight. Heavy crystal paperweight with interior threads of white glass swirling around a trapped air bubble, 3 inches diameter. (Photograph courtesy of Steuben Glass.)

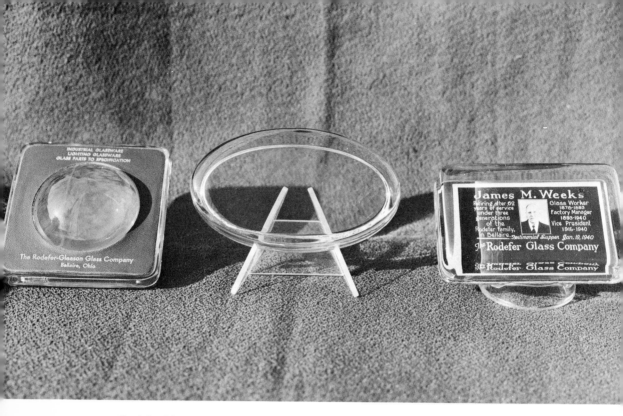

Rodefer-Gleason Glass Company paperweights. *Left to right:* Weight with magnifying lens; oval flow weight; commemorative pressed weight. (Photograph by George J. Melvin.)

five-petal flowers and some with three or four flowers per weight. Three were made with three flowers (one red, one white, one blue) and five weights were made with two similar flowers enclosed: two weights with two red flowers, two with two blue flowers, one with one blue and one red flower.

Rodefer-Gleason Glass Company eagle weight. Design was pressed, then etched to give frosted appearance. Weight is from the collection of Mrs. Sanford Finder. (Photograph by George J. Melvin.)

Floated Weights

If the reader has questioned, as did the author, where the commercial rectangular- and oval-shaped crystal paperweights are made—that is, the kind one pastes family portraits behind—the answer is found in the Rodefer-Gleason Glass Company of Bellaire, Ohio. This is one of several factories making floated or pressed crystal weights. Twenty-three varieties were made at one time by this company, in various weights ranging from 7½ ounces to 13 ounces in shapes including circles, squares, domes, ovals, rectangles, and one unusual round with an eagle design etched into the undersurface.

A visit to this factory to see floated weights in the making proved very interesting. Six oval molds are placed on a round, rotating metal plate. A shop of four workers turns out five hundred floated weights per turn (one-half working day). The gatherer places the hot metal over the oval mold where the presser shears off a carefully estimated amount of glass to flow into the mold, while the take-out boy spreads another cooling mold and removes and transfers to scales the oval shape. Then the form, if perfect in shape and correct in weight is transferred to an asbestos pad on a carry-in pole and carried with three similar weights to the lehr for gradual annealing and cooling.

In addition to the floated weights Rodefer-Gleason also runs an infrequent turn of pressed crystal weights. This requires the same number of workers in a shop as the floated weights—the gatherer, the presser, the

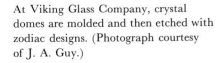

At Viking Glass Company, crystal domes are molded and then etched with zodiac designs. (Photograph courtesy of J. A. Guy.)

Floated weights. Made by shearing off a gather into a metal mold by gravity flow. The examples are a Clevenger Brothers frog and a Cambridge Glass Works bird. (Photograph by the author.)

take-out boy, and the carry-in boy. Pressed weights have a very distinctive edge on the inside, up to 3/32 inch deep, where the plunger leaves a sharper edge. Pressed weights must be fire-polished to have a smooth top surface, whereas floated weights are usually very smooth, clear, and free from flaws.

It is difficult for factories making these commercial weights by floating or pressing to compete with other factories where, through automation, fifty weights a minute can be stamped out on a rotary table. The owners of floated weights should treasure them for what they are, because the time will come when no more are available.

Until the days of competition from automation, the Rodefer-Gleason Glass Company ran two or three shops daily in weight making. This factory at Bellaire, Ohio, has the distinction of being the oldest glass factory in the United States operating continuously in the same location. It was founded in 1877.

Bells. Bell-shaped paperweights have been made at several factories including Rodefer-Gleason and Fenton Art Glass. (Photograph by the author.)

Collectors may be interested to note that Mr. Rodefer identified some of the small, blue glass, bell-shaped paperweights as a product of this factory.

Fenton Art Glass Company, Williamstown, West Virginia

During a visit to the Fenton Art Glass Company, Williamstown, West Virginia, Mr. Frank Fenton, President, permitted me to photograph his office doorstop. It is very beautifully crafted, the work of Peter Raymond, the man responsible for one of Fenton's glass decorative processes. Mr. Fenton advised me that a light blue paperweight bell, which reads on one side "Save Time Telephone" and on the reverse side "Save Steps Telephone," was made at Fenton. A deeper cobalt blue bell weight of the same design was crafted at Fenton much earlier, perhaps during the 1930's.

Chapter 28

Customs of

Former Years

Research for a book such as this reveals much of interest in the history of glass factories and in the customs of these factories. In talking with older glassworkers now retired who had experience working in these factories at the turn of the century, I learned some facts which I believe are worth passing along.

Almost without exception the early glass factories permitted their employees, the gaffers especially, to make offhand glass pieces experimentally when a day's work was completed. Some of this after-hours work was devoted to paperweights, not as production items, but rather as gifts for the maker's friends or as gifts to those who had favored him. The paperweights of this earlier time were usually made by workers who had observed or had been trained by the glassworkers who immigrated from Europe—principally France, Belgium, Italy, Switzerland, and later Czechoslovakia. Many of the fine older American weights in contemporary collections were undoubtedly made by those immigrant glassworkers or others who copied their style. Some immigrant workers brought with them both glassmaking tools and the all-important glass canes, threads, and other types of design items to incorporate in these weights.

As John Fischer, the retired glass gaffer of the Duncan Miller Glass Company, explained to me, "It is most difficult to credit some glass prod-

Pictured is a shop at work in about 1913 at the McDonald, Pennsylvania glass plant known as the Crescent Bottle Company. This company established in 1899 opened a newly constructed plant with a fourteen pot furnace in 1900. The chief products were druggists' and perfumers' flint glass bottles. Introduction of the automatic bottle pressing machine spelled the doom of the factory which closed in 1927. (Photo furnished by Mrs. Ruth S. Miller of McDonald, Pa. Photo by Lewis Studio, McDonald, Pa.)

ucts to any certain factory or worker because some of the most skilled of these early glassmen skipped about the country constantly. They took their tools and cane-filled suitcases to one factory, worked a time, and as was the case with many of these early glass-factory workers, drank considerable whisky after each payday. In their drunken state the working conditions at some distant factory always seemed more attractive, so with tools and suitcase in hand, they progressed to some other glass center— to work only until the notion struck them to move again." These workers were said to have "ridden the rods" in some instances.

The young boy training into glasswork must certainly have been endowed with great fortitude. John Fischer said it was a common practice of some gaffers to "rough up" the carry-in boy or the bit boy. Another of our present-day glass weight makers said that as an apprentice he would feel the burn from the hot glass bit the gaffer would swing his way to torment him on occasion. One of our retired weight makers remembers that young boys learning glasswork were knocked down by the gaffer if the glass production in process was not judged good enough. The glassworker of this past era must have been the hardheaded, hardworking, hard-to-please man he is credited with being by so many experienced in working with him.

John Fischer said a common practice in some glasshouses was to fill an emptied whisky barrel with water, put in a big chunk of ice, and hang the dipper beside it. Thus the glassworkers enjoyed whisky-flavored water during working hours. During his apprenticeship, Fischer was sent by his gaffer one hot evening to a nearby beer parlor for a tin dinner pail of beer. Some token was always carried to identify the intended consumer as no money exchanged hands for the beer. The drink was charged to the account of the glassworker until payday when the bartender collected his dues. John Fischer showed the token and returned to climb over the wall of the factory with the filled pail, only to drop into the arms of the factory owner, Mr. Duncan. While Mr. Duncan scolded the boy, he really took the gaffer to task for sending his apprentice on such an errand during working hours —against factory rules. John Fischer said he was never asked to do this trick again—though this did not stop the practice among other gaffers.

Wages paid these boy apprentice glassworkers were very meager. I heard a story of two young glassworkers who had only one pair of shoes between them, so one lad worked days while the other worked nights.

What of the future of paperweights? As the years pass, there will be, in all probability, paperweight collectors. Some economically independent collectors will scramble at each auction for the beautifully crafted foreign weights. Perhaps some collectors will be content with the less costly American-made weights of the 1960's. A discriminating buyer can and should find some of the present-day weights a pleasant addition to his collection.

Judging from the rapid rise in prices reported on weight sales at home and abroad in the year 1964, one can scarcely question the wisdom of collecting both well-crafted contemporary weights and the fine older weights.

UNITED STATES PATENT OFFICE.

HENRY D. HOLLOWAY AND FREDERICK W. RHODES, OF KANSAS CITY, MISSOURI.

PAPER-WEIGHT.

SPECIFICATION forming part of Letters Patent No. 560,502, dated May 19, 1896.

Application filed March 13, 1896. Serial No. 583,084. (No model.)

To all whom it may concern:

Be it known that we, HENRY D. HOLLOWAY and FREDERICK W. RHODES, citizens of the United States, residing at Kansas City, in the county of Jackson and State of Missouri, have invented certain new and useful Improvements in Paper-Weights; and we do hereby declare the following to be a full, clear, and exact description of the invention, such as will enable others skilled in the art to which it appertains to make and use the same.

Our invention relates to improvements in paper-weights, and more particularly to that class known as "pen racks and cleaners," the object being to combine in one article a suitable pen-rack, pen-cleaner, pincushion, and the whole to be a handy and useful paper-weight with novel means for retaining the inserted pens immovably in the position which they originally assume. This is essential where a paper-weight is to be also a pen holder or rack, as a wabbling or falling out of the said pens would render it useless as a weight.

With these and other objects and advantages in view our invention consists in certain new and novel features of construction hereinafter fully described, and particularly pointed out in the hereto-annexed claims made a part of this specification.

In the accompanying drawings, clearly illustrating our invention, Figure 1 is a transverse sectional view of the combined paper-weight, pen-rack, pen-cleaner, and pincushion; Fig. 2 is a plan view of the same.

Like numerals of reference designate like parts in both figures of the drawings.

We construct the weight 1 with a reservoir or hollow interior 2 and pen-openings in any number desired leading down into said reservoir. We have shown three of these openings 3, and preferably situate them at diametrically opposite points near the periphery of the globular dome of the weight. This construction or form of the dome, approximately spherical, directs the pens inserted in the pen-openings 3 toward a central point near the base of the weight. Here the pen-points are inserted in shot 4, with which the reservoir is partially filled, or in any other suitable material of a disintegrated state and designed to afford a yielding and cleansing seat for their reception.

Depending centrally from the interior of the dome and extending to or near the base of the weight 1 is a core 5, whose general form is that of a cone with a convex surface. The purpose and function of this construction of the interior of the weight with a conical or approximately conical depending core will be readily apparent upon examination of Fig. 1 of the drawings, where it will be noted that the pens are guided to and rest against this core by reason of the shape of the dome and the relatively-situated pen-openings 3. Were it not for the core located centrally in the reservoir 2 the pens would at each moving of the weight shift their position and finally become displaced. This would interfere with the usefulness of the pen-rack as a paper-weight and place the manuscript to be weighted in jeopardy of ink-blots. As it is, the pens remain immovably in their original position, and such stabili... ...ly to the above-described c... ...r of the exterior surf... ...l, as at 6, and in... ...ner or wiper 7, ...itable wiping ...site one of the ...3, seated in a ...ed to the sur-

...ly construct ...ich can read- ...shion can be ...d a reservoir ...suitable cover. ...cate the approxi- ...shion and ink-well sho... ...bined with the paper-weight.

The weight may be constructed of any suitable material—such as glass, aluminium, hard rubber, or wood—and the shape or design may suit the individual fancy. The dome does not of necessity require to be formed spherically, but may be flat, the essential part being to so incline the axes of the pen-openings as to direct the pens toward a central point.

We do not desire to confine ourselves to the precise details of construction herein shown

Chapter 29

Paperweight

Patents

The study of United States patents pertinent to the manufacture of paperweights is a most interesting one which affords an occasional smile. Patented weights may be constructed of glass, of metal, and more recently of plastic.

Many patents were granted to inventors who combined the use of paperweights with some other desk duty, such as pen holders, pen racks, pincushions, knife rests, (one wonders what executives kept carving knives on their desks), current or perpetual calendars (W. Bright, 1901), magnifying-glass weights to read individual lines of fine print, and memorandum weights which were both lined and etched to accommodate penciled notes. (The notes once used were erased by rubbing off with a wet finger or damp cloth, L. B. Martin, 1891.) Other patented designs include a weight which was also a miniature hourglass-type timepiece (L. L. Doolittle, 1911), one which was a bank, and two weights which were display containers for specimens of natural products. Of course, many patents were granted to weight inventors who would include portraits (J. B. Wilson, 1872) or advertising lettering, decals, or pictures in the base or sometimes in a raised integral angular glass frame. One would be hard pressed to keep up with the ever-changing postal rates of today—but in days past a schedule of postal rates appeared as a design in commercial weights distributed as an advertising medium.

It might be reasonable to guess that the forerunner of today's popular pencil-holder paperweights made by John Gentile, Joe Zimmerman, and Ray Stone was the 1896 patent to Holloway and Rhodes for a paperweight which held steel pen points in holders, a pen-point cleaner in the top of the hemisphere, and a pincushion or inkwell in the sides of the weight.

Patents were granted to inventors for a widely varying number of ideas, but the majority appear to be improvements on some prior design. The patents researched extend from 1872 to the present year.

Missing from patents granted are designs for many of the well-known flower-design weights made in the United States. Perhaps the lack of patents on designs accounts for so many similar designs being made by gaffers in widely separated glass manufacturing centers. Of course, the frequent removal of these craftsmen from one factory to another no doubt contributed even more to the exchange and spread of many popular paperweight designs.

The most frequently collected American paperweight designs which are patented include those pictured: H. Miller, Glass Paperweight, May 27, 1890; H. E. Geron, Turtle with moving parts, May 18, 1948; J. G. Funfrock, Bird design, March 30, 1948; J. G. Funfrock, Butterfly design, March 30, 1948.

Both of the last two patent rights were purchased by Peter Gentile, and the designs shown are being manufactured today by his son, John Gentile.

If a collector were to attempt to secure one example of each paperweight patented, he would most certainly have an interesting and extended journey within our United States. Patented or not, collecting American-made paper-weights is a fascinating hobby. Good hunting!

An early paperweight patent of 1872 granted to James Bernard Wilson of Philadelphia, Pennsylvania combined an ornamented metal frame formed with a lip to permit the insertion of a glass plate. After the application of a picture or an advertisement to the under side of the glass the weight was completed with a layer of plaster of paris.

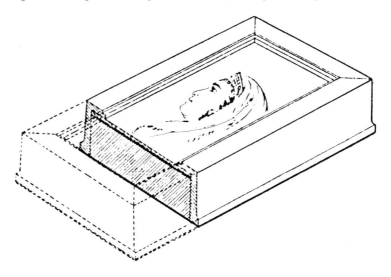

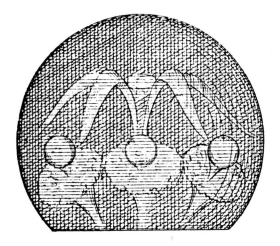

Henry Miller's paperweight design patented in 1890 was a glass sphere flattened on one side which contained one large center flower surrounded by smaller flowers grouped around and below. Each flower was provided with a bulbous pistil. This Pittsburgher's idea is copied even today, attesting to the popularity of the design.

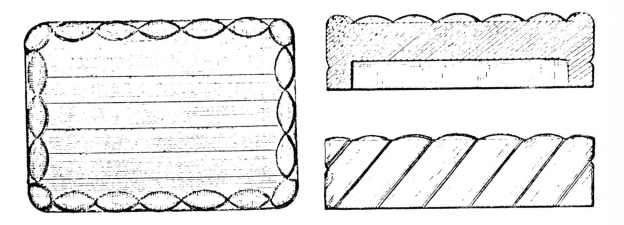

Lucien B. Martin of Fostoria, Ohio, proposed a three-purpose product. His patent of 1891 combined a design of glass heavy enough to serve as a paperweight with an acid etched top surface which permitted a memoranda of penciled notes (to be erased with a dampened finger when no longer needed). The cavity at the bottom of the design permitted a calendar or an advertisement to be inserted.

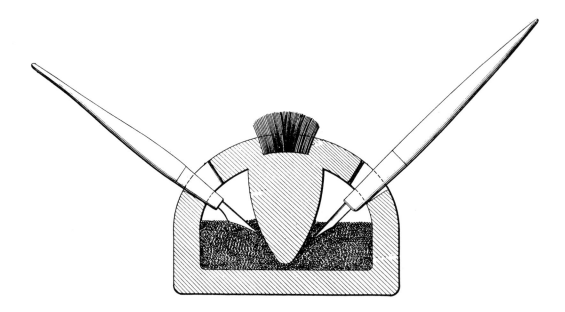

In May 1896 was patented a combination pen-holder, pen-cleaner, pin-cushion paperweight. Pens inserted in the reservoir were retained immovable in the position which they originally assumed. This patent was granted to Henry D. Holloway and Frederick W. Rhodes of Kansas City, Missouri.

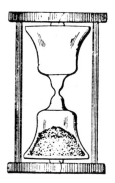

Laura Leggett Doolittle of New Haven, Connecticut, patented in July 1911 an ornamental design for a paperweight and a time piece. Two transparent bell shapes were joined to make a time piece contained within a rigid frame of sufficient weight to become a paperweight.

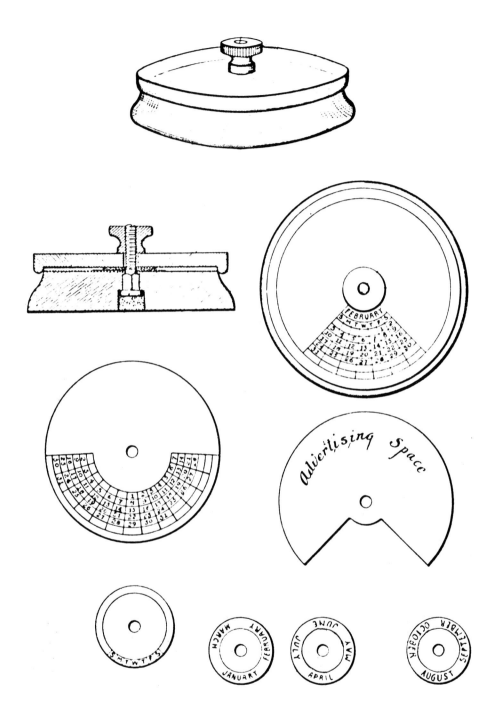

William Bright of St. Louis, Missouri, in 1901 patented a glass enclosed, calendar paper-weight. Revolving disks permitted the viewing of the current month and day with ample space left on the top disk for an advertisement.

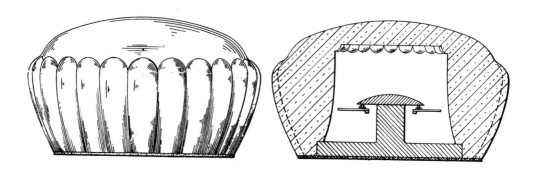

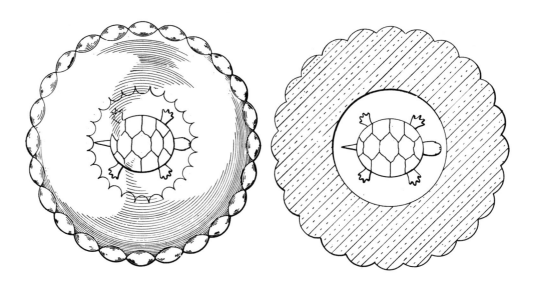

The popular turtle with movable parts was patented by Harry E. Geron of Springfield, Ohio, in May 1948.

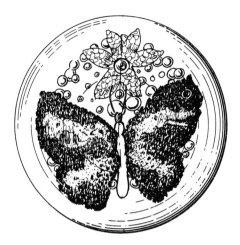

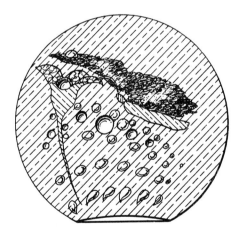

A design for a transparent glass paperweight containing a butterfly and flower design was patented by John G. Funfrock in 1948. This design was first crafted by Peter Gentile in his factory at Star City, West Virginia, at the time he and Mr. Funfrock were partners in the G. and F. Glass Co.

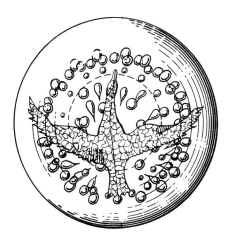
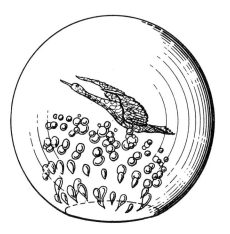
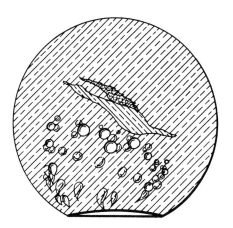

A transparent paperweight design containing a flying goose was patented by John G. Funfrock in 1948. This design was crafted by Peter Gentile in his factory at Star City, West Virginia.

Chapter 30

Glossary

air trap- interior weight bubble between layers of glass

anneal- to gradual reduce glass temperature in an oven, lehr, or muffle

base- bottom of a paperweight

base color- layer of color closest to the weight bottom

batch- mixture of ingredients to melt in glass furnace

block- hollowed apple- or cherry-wood tool used to shape crown of paperweight

breakoff- rough area of glass at base of weight left when pontil is broken off; act of striking weight from pontil by sharp blow to pontil

bubble mold- a hollow, metal-hinged mold with evenly spaced interior spikes used to create minute air traps in weights

cane- slices or segments of a glass rod used at random or in careful setups for interior motif of paperweight. Types: candy (broken) millefiori, silhouette, filigree

collar- metal cylinder used to surround die (design) plate

cookie base- a flat, circular pad of crystal used as a weight rest (for John Gentile's blown apple and pear paperweights)

cords- undesirable fine or wavy lines apparent in the metal of some paperweights; also called *striae*

crimp- a metal tool inserted to model color within a weight to form raised sections and also three dimensional roses

crown- final gather of glass which is blocked to enclose design

cullet- broken glass remnants often used in small portions to help fuse a new batch

cup- see *collar*

cushion- a paperweight ground which is convex in form

cutting- exterior decorative motifs added to weights by use of abrasives and wheel grinding to make facets, punties, and miter cuts

cut-down tools- metal tools used to reduce size of glass gather at pontil breakoff point; also called *pucellas*

design- interior motif in paperweight

Devil's fire weight- design of swirling glass color

diameter- most widely used measurement in weight description

die- design incised in metal plate

dome- tapered cylindrical weight

doorstop- a very large weight, 5 inches or over in diameter

Bibliography

BERGSTROM, EVANGELINE H., *Old Glass Paperweights.* New York: Crown Publishers, Inc., 1947.

BERGSTROM, EVANGELINE H., "Steeple Weights," Paperweight Collectors Round-Up, *Hobbies,* XLVI, No. 8 (October, 1941), 73.

BIBB, JUNE, "Deft Hands Turn Glass Peppermint Sticks into Art," *The Christian Science Monitor,* LVI, No. 307 (November 24, 1964), 9.

BLACKISTONE, Z. D., JR., "The Cumberland Glass Story," *Spinning Wheel,* XVII, No. 10 (October, 1962), 14–16.

BOORE, J. P., "Glass Paperweights," *Hobbies,* LXIII, No. 5 (July, 1958), 76; LXIII, No. 6 (August, 1958), 80; LXIII, No. 7 (September, 1958), 82; LXIII, No. 8 (October, 1958), 72; LXIII, No. 9 (November, 1958), 82; LXIII, No. 10 (December, 1958), 72; LXIII, No. 11 (January, 1959), 72; LXIII, No. 12 (February, 1959), 72; LXIV, No. 1 (March, 1959), 72; LXIV, No. 2 (April, 1959), 72.

BOZEK, MICHAEL, "Paperweights," *Treasure Chest,* I, No. 3 (May–June, 1961), 20.

BOZEK, MICHAEL, *Price Guide Handbook of Glass Paperweights.* North Hollywood, California: Treasure Chest Publications, 1961.

BROTHERS, J. STANLEY, JR., "The Miracle of Enclosed Ornamentation," *Journal of Glass Studies,* Corning, New York: The Corning Museum of Glass, IV, (1962), 116–126.

BUEHR, WALTER, *The Marvel of Glass.* New York: William Morrow and Company, 1963.

Bulletin of the Paperweight Collectors' Association. Scarsdale, New York: By Paul Jokelson, 1956, 1957, 1959, 1960, 1961, 1962, 1963, 1964, 1965.

China Glass and Tablewares. Redbook Directory Issue. Indiantown, Florida: Ebel-Doctorow Publications, Inc., LXXXI, No. 6 (May 15, 1963).

DREPPERD, CARL W., *A Dictionary of American Antiques.* Boston: Charles T. Branford Company, 1952.

ELVILLE, E. M., *Paperweights and Other Glass Curiosities.* London: Country Life Limited, 1954.

Epstein, Sam and Beryl, *The First Book of Glass.* New York: Franklin Watts, Inc., 1955.

Gaines, Edith, "Woman's Day Dictionary of American Glass," *Woman's Day,* Greenwich, Connecticut: Fawcett Publications, Inc., (August, 1961), 19.

Gasparetto, Astone, and Van Saldern, Alex, "Glass," *Encyclopedia of World Art,* London: McGraw-Hill Publishing Company, VI, 1962, p. 389.

The Glass Club Bulletin. Organ of the National Early American Glass Club, No. 6 (February, 1940); No. 7 (June, 1940); No. 37 (December, 1954); No. 38 (September, 1955); No. 45 (March, 1958); No. 70 (June, 1964).

"Glass-Dancing Lights for Party Tables," *House and Garden,* Greenwich, Connecticut: Condé Nast Publications, Inc., CXXVII, No. 3 (February, 1965), 113–115.

Green, Doris M., "Paperweights and Pieces on Paperweight Technique," *Spinning Wheel,* XII, No. 4, (April, 1956), 10, 11.

Gunther, Charles F., "Glass Blowing in the Classroom," *School Arts,* LXIV, No. 5 (January, 1965), 29–32.

Herrick, Ruth M. D., *Greentown Glass.* Greentown, Indiana: By the Author, 1959.

Jenkins, Dorothy H., "The Spell of Paperweights," *Woman's Day,* Greenwich, Connecticut: Fawcett Publications, Inc. (February, 1965), 12.

Jenkins, Dorothy H., "Woman's Day Dictionary of Paperweights," *Woman's Day,* Greenwich, Connecticut: Fawcett Publications, Inc. (July, 1965), 25–32.

Johnson, Grace, "Old Paperweights," *Hobbies,* LI, No. 4 (May, 1946), 53, 54.

Jokelson, Paul, *Antique French Glass Paperweights.* Scarsdale, New York: By the Author, 1955.

Kiener, C. A., "English Green Glass Paperweights," *Hobbies,* XLIV, No. 8 (October, 1941), 71.

Knittle, Rhea Mansfield, *Early American Glass.* New York: Garden City Publishing Company, 1927.

Laing, Robert Clark Estate, *Glass Paperweight Auction,* Sale # 1669, New York: Catalogue of Parke-Bernet Galleries, Inc., 1956.

"Lamp Working," *American Flint,* Toledo, Ohio: American Flint Glass Workers Union of North America, L, No. 3 (March, 1960), 12.

Lee, Ruth Webb, *Antique Fakes and Reproductions.* New York: Ferris Printing Company, By the Author, 1938.

Lee, Ruth Webb, "Medium Priced Paperweights," Paperweight Collectors Round-Up, *Hobbies,* XLVI, No. 8 (October, 1941), 59.

Leffingwell, B. H., "Paperweights for the Advanced Collector," *The Antiques Journal,* Uniontown, Pennsylvania: II, No. 3 (March, 1964), 20–22.

LEONARDSON, S. E., "Fowlerton Paperweights, B. F. Leach Glass Company," *Hobbies,* XLVIII, No. 12 (February, 1944), 50–54.

LINDSEY, BESSIE M., *Lore of Our Land Pictured in Glass.* I, II, Waganer Printing Company, By the Author, 1948.

LYON, H. M., "Ravenna, Ohio Glass," *Hobbies,* XLIV, No. 12 (February, 1940), 51–53.

McKEARIN, GEORGE S. AND HELEN, *American Glass.* New York: Crown Publishers, Inc., 1941.

McKEARIN, HELEN AND GEORGE S., *Two Hundred Years of American Blown Glass.* New York: Crown Publishers, Inc., 1949.

MARSH, TRACY H., *The American Story Recorded in Glass.* Minneapolis, Minnesota: Lund Press, Inc., By the Author, 1962.

MOORE, T. B., "The First Hundred Are the Easiest," Paperweight Collectors Round-Up, *Hobbies,* XLVI, No. 8 (October, 1941), 68.

New England Glass Company 1818–1888. Toledo, Ohio: Toledo Museum of Art, 1963.

PHILLIPS, C. J., *Glass: The Miracle Maker.* New York: Pitman Publishing Company, 1941.

REVELLI, YVONNE, "Thoughts on French Paperweights," Paperweight Collectors Round-Up, *Hobbies,* XLVI, No. 8 (October, 1941), 70, 71.

REVI, ALBERT CHRISTIAN, *Nineteenth Century Glass: Its Genesis and Development.* New York: Thomas Nelson and Sons, 1959.

SHELLEY, DONALD A., "Henry Ford and the Museum," Glass-Illustration Number 19 Paperweights, *Antiques,* LXXIII, No. 2 (February, 1958), 148.

"The Silica Sands of Ottawa," *Hi-Lines,* Decatur, Illinois: Illinois Power Company (February, 1964), 11.

SMITH, DIDO, "Offhand Glass Blowing," *Craft Horizons,* XXIV, No. 1, (January/February, 1964), 90, 91.

SMITH, FRANCIS EDGAR, *American Glass Paperweights.* Wollaston, Massachusetts: The Antique Press, 1939.

The Story of Steuben Glass. Corning, New York: Steuben Glass, 1964.

SVERBEYEFF, ELIZABETH, "Out in the Open," *The New York Times Magazine,* April 18, 1965, pp. 90, 91.

SWIFT, CAROLINE HYDE, "Charles Kaziun," *Bulletin of Paperweight Collectors' Association,* II, No. 1.

THACHER, THURSTON, "Incognito Collectors and Collections," Paperweight Collectors Round-Up, *Hobbies,* XLVI, No. 8 (October, 1941), 61.

"Treasures in Trunks," *Time,* LXII (July 6, 1953), 56.

WATKINS, LAURA WOODSIDE, *Cambridge Glass 1818–1888.* Boston: Marshall Jones Company, 1930.

WILSON, KENNETH M., "The Mount Washington Glass Works and Its Successors 1837–1958," *Antiques,* LXXIV, No. 1 (July, 1958), 46.

WINCHESTER, ALICE, *The Antiques Book.* Chapter V, "Old Glass Paperweights," Mary A. and S. Weldon O'Brien, New York: Bonanza Books, Crown Publishers, 1950, pp. 202–208.

YEAGER, DOROTHEA, "Comments on Paperweights," Paperweight Collectors Round-Up, *Hobbies,* XLVI, No. 8 (October, 1941), 62.

Index

Index of Weights

Key: Each weight (listed by the name given by the maker) is keyed to the maker according to the following list. Italic page numbers indicate illustrations; P signifies color plate page.

JB	Joseph Barker	Ko	Edward Koztoski
WB	William Breeden	EK	Emil Kuhn
ZB	Zack Boyd	JK	John Kreutz
WC	William Claytor	L	Emil Larson
D	John, Charles, and William	Li	Harvey K. Littleton
	Degenhart	DL	Dominick Labino
Di	John DiBella	M	Otto Macho
E	Carl Erickson	JM	John Murphy
G	Gentile family	RM	Robert Moretti
JG	John Gentile	TM	Tom Mosser
PG	Peter Gentile	PN	Patrick Naples
H	Gus Hofbauer	R	Edward Rithner
FH	Frank Hamilton	Ra	Peter Raymond
HH	Harold Hacker	S	Jonathan R. Stone
JH	James Hamilton	St	Steuben Glass
RH	Ronald Hansen	StC	St. Clair Glass Works
Ham	Robert Hamon	SZ	Alex Stelzer
OHam	O. C. Hamon	W	Francis Whittemore
I	William Iorio	CW	Charles Windsor
HJ	Henry Johnson	X	Harry Caralluzzo
K	Charles Kaziun	Z	Zimmerman Art Glass
		Zi	William Zick, Jr. and Sr.

A & W Root Beer, 144
Air twist, (CW), 241
Animals, 225, 226
  (K), 196
  (D), *P6*
  (Z), *P1*
  (ZB), *P1*
  (HH), *P5*
  (W), 206
  (PN), 233
Apples, (StC), 140, *236, P14*
  (Z), *149,* 151, *P11*
Aster, (Z), 150

"Atlantic City, New Jersey,"
  (G), 71

Bee, (D), *49*
Bell weights, 254, 255
  (StC), *141, P1, P6, P14*
  (Z), 153
  (JG), *P6*
  (R), *P8*
Bird, white, (R), *129*
Black Diamond, (ZB), 214
Bubble weights, (E), *58*
  (D), 55

(G), *71*
(StC), *141*
(JH), 223
(Z), *P11*
(PN), 233
(E), *P19*
(X), 216
Bug, (G), *P6*
Butterfly, (D), *49,* 53
  (PG) *64, P19*
  (JG), *67,* 76, *P10*
  (G), 71
  (M), 115

DATE DUE

NOV 11 1995			

Tools of the Trade